MAYBECK'S LANDSCAPES

MAYBECK'S LANDSCAPES

DRAWING IN NATURE

DIANNE HARRIS

Berkeley/Design/Books #1

WILLIAM STOUT
PUBLISHERS
SAN FRANCISCO

This book was published with the assistance of
The Getty Foundation and
the Graham Foundation for Advanced Studies
in the Fine Arts.

Published in cooperation with the
College of Environmental Design,
University of California, Berkeley

Berkeley/Design/Books promote historical and critical scholarship on subjects drawn from the Environmental Design Archives at the University of California, Berkeley. One of the nation's premier design archives, its collections hold graphic materials, written documents, and personal papers concerning American and foreign architecture, landscape architecture, and planning.

Marc Treib, Series Editor
Waverly Lowell, Curator, Environmental Design Archives

ISBN 0974621404
Library of Congress Control Number 2005922557

Designed by Marc Treib

Published by
William Stout Publishers
530 Greenwich Street
San Francisco, California 94133
www.stoutbooks.com

Printed in China

For Marc Treib

FRONTISPIECE

ROSE WALK (?), BERKELEY, 1912. PASTEL STUDY.
[ENVIRONMENTAL DESIGN ARCHIVES,
UNIVERSITY OF CALIFORNIA, BERKELEY]

CONTENTS

PREFACE AND ACKNOWLEDGMENTS

This study began as a brief paper written for a seminar on the relationship of building, garden, and landscape, taught by Marc Treib in the fall of 1988. At that time, I was a student in the University of California, Berkeley's Master's of Architecture program. Having obtained an undergraduate degree in landscape architecture in 1983, I was, at that time, deeply interested in the range of relationships that could be formulated between architecture and its surroundings. Through a stroke of good fortune, I was also employed during those years (1987–89) as the student archivist in the College of Environmental Design Archives, where Bernard Maybeck's papers are housed. During my spare time (what little there was of it), I seized the opportunity to study as many of the Collection's drawings as possible. As I examined sheet after sheet of Maybeck's drawings, I became increasingly intrigued. The richness and exuberance of his landscape designs, which seemed to fill the pages of his drawings, both inspired and captivated my attention. I was certainly aware of Maybeck's architectural reputation but had never read anything about his interest in integrating landscape into his schemes. How had the architect learned about landscape design and why was there so much landscape imagery drawn onto the pages of his presentation drawings, sketches, and designs of all sorts? What was his approach to landscape design, and how were his landscape schemes related to his architectural works? The questions those renderings generated then became central to the formation of my Master's thesis, completed in 1989.[1]

Although some years have passed since I first began that project, the questions surrounding the landscape/architecture interface have remained compelling. As an historian, my studies moved away from the exploration of the works of specific designers, but since I still occasionally teach design courses in landscape architecture and participate in studio reviews, the questions raised by my thesis research still seem relevant for students and practitioners alike. That Maybeck was highly skilled at both the design of buildings and landscapes is somewhat unusual; designers who have worked in both realms are aware of the diverse proficiencies required by each, and it remains relatively rare to find professionals who are equally skilled in both landscape and architectural design. It is true that many architects of Maybeck's era included landscape in renderings as a visual commonplace — what art historians call "staffage" and architects sometimes call "entourage" — and they frequently acted as landscape designers for their projects while the profession of landscape architecture was still in its infancy with relatively few practitioners nationwide.[2] Yet Maybeck's deeply integrative method remains unusual, as I will demonstrate in the pages that follow. Using a range of approaches rather than any unified formal or stylistic doctrine, Maybeck's work presents one method for resolving the treatment of the common ground shared by architecture and landscape.

Since this project's inception, numerous detailed studies on nineteenth- and twentieth-century North American landscape architecture and designers have emerged. For example, monographs on Jens Jensen, Alfred Caldwell, and detailed essays on a range of Midwestern and other regional designers now exist, making my task easier than it once was. Although I will briefly compare Maybeck's landscapes with some other designers from his period, this is not a book about turn-of-the-century landscape architecture in the United States or on the West Coast. Rather than repeat the information found in these recent and very useful texts, I refer the reader to them.[3]

For historians, this book contributes to the scholarship on Maybeck and early Bay Region architecture, and similarly indicates the rewards of examining architecture and landscape in tandem, and in context.[4] Throughout, I assume a certain familiarity on the part of the reader with Maybeck's architectural works, which have been the subject of significant scholarly publications by Kenneth Cardwell, William Jordy, Richard Longstreth, and Sally Woodbridge, among others.[5] Many of Maybeck's designs included landscapes or gardens — indeed, few of his design development drawings exclude some delineation of landscape. The architect made these drawings using various media and techniques, but he favored (and was highly skilled in creating) freehand sketches made with colored pastel on large sheets of brown kraft paper or on yellow tracing paper. For presentation renderings he sometimes substituted gouache for chalk, but the brown paper remained his preferred "canvas." When they can be found, planting schemes appear in pencil (colored and not) on yellow tracing paper, and the margins of such plans sometimes contain colored pencil sketches that further reveal the designer's intention. A few planting schemes appear on construction documents, but the bulk of the evidence for this book derives from design development drawings, presentation renderings, and written documents in project files. Maybeck produced designs using plan, section, elevation, perspective, and aerial or birds-eye views, choosing the means that best served his objectives. No matter what the format, landscape appears consistently, even when the inclusion seems gratuitous given the intent of the drawing. I selected the projects presented herein for their relevance to the subject at hand and for the availability of information regarding those projects.[6] Whenever possible, I have also examined the sites of built projects where remnants of Maybeck's landscape schemes remain visible.

This book comprises two parts. The first section summarizes Maybeck's education and the influences that shaped his design method. It also places his work within the context of Northern California at the turn of the twentieth century. The second section provides a more detailed analysis of the architect's integrative strategies by examining specific projects in greater depth and detail.

Many people generously contributed time, attention, and resources that were invaluable to my work on this project over the years. Marc Treib was present at this study's inception and served as chair of my thesis committee. He helped with my first publications which were on this topic, and now—as editor of this series—he is responsible for its final publication in book form. His unflagging encouragement and enthusiasm for this project (and others over the years) have been as important as his excellent editorial comments, creative input, and intelligent criticism. His sharp wit and sharper eye never cease to amuse and amaze me, and I am tremendously grateful for his help on this and many other projects. Dell Upton and Richard Peters also served on the thesis committee. Dell was particularly influential in determining the direction of this project in its earliest phase, helping to formulate a historical context for it, and Richard Peters's interest in the topic proved contagious. Stephen Tobriner granted the great gift of access to the materials in the Documents Collection, today known as the Environmental Design Archives. Without his trust and guidance, this project would not have happened. Margaretta Lovell and the members of the 1988 noon hour workshops she hosted gave useful commentary and criticism on the preliminary paper that became this thesis, particularly Mark Brack, Bruno Giberti, and Annmarie Adams. The late David Gebhard generously read and commented on the thesis just after it was completed in 1989, as did Kenneth Cardwell, who also shared key insights during a telephone interview. John Dixon Hunt published my first article on this topic (also my first ever publication) in *The Journal of Garden History*, and Therese O'Malley asked important questions that led to the refinement of some key ideas for my essay on this topic published in *Regional Garden Design in the United States*. Nicholas Adams and Richard Longstreth critically reviewed the manuscript and offered excellent suggestions for improvement, for which I am most grateful.

Edith Gladstone edited with alacrity; Karen Madsen and Carrie McDade provided excellent proofreading. My thanks also to David Hays for emergency photographic assistance from Paris.

The late Jacomena Maybeck, Bernard Maybeck's daughter-in-law, gave valuable information and generously loaned slides in 1988. Dr. Leslie Roos patiently answered all my questions and located the photographs of the original Roos garden. Mr. and Mrs. Trinkl, owners of the Senger residence, graciously allowed me to study and photograph their house and garden. Waverly Lowell, with Carrie McDade, has transformed the Environmental Design Archives from a shoe-string operation into one of the finest and best-organized archives of architectural and landscape drawings in the United States—no small task considering the limited funding available. I thank them not only for their assistance, but also for their hard work and persistent efforts to build and preserve this valuable resource for all of us who care about the history of the built environment. My mother, Charlotte Johnston, patiently introduced me to word processing as I (a late convert from the typewriter) wrote the Maybeck thesis on her computer in 1988–89. For her generosity and support, I thank her again here. Finally, my thanks, as always, to my husband Lawrence Hamlin and to my daughter Madeleine for the everyday support, good humor, and for the encouragement to get the job done.

Centuries ago, before the modern age of advanced specialization was dreamed of, had an architect been asked to create an exposition, he would have been not only an architect, but a painter, sculptor, and landscape engineer as well. He would have thought, planned and executed from this fourfold angle, and I doubt if it would have even occurred to him to think of one of the arts as detached from another.

George Kelham, Chief of Exposition Architecture, Panama Pacific International Exposition, circa. 1915.

FIGURE 1

BERNARD MAYBECK, UNDATED.

[ENVIRONMENTAL DESIGN ARCHIVES, UNIVERSITY OF CALIFORNIA, BERKELEY, HEREAFTER EDA, UCB]

MAYBECK'S LANDSCAPES

At the beginning of the twentieth century, the members of Berkeley's Hillside Club proclaimed that "hillside architecture is landscape gardening around a few rooms for use in case of rain."[7] As residents of the Berkeley hills concerned about the development of an East Bay neighborhood culture, the club members often addressed questions of environmental design. Among the most well known of this group's proclamations, the above quotation frequently appears in architectural histories of the early San Francisco Bay Region. Although applicable to the work of many of the early practitioners, the statement most accurately describes the work of Bernard Ralph Maybeck (1862–1957), whose architecture, regardless of scale or type, uniformly and richly incorporated designed landscapes throughout the long span of his career (1890s–1940) [figure 1]. Generally acknowledged as one of the key ingredients in the success of Maybeck's architecture, the integral relation of his buildings to their landscape surroundings and the importance of this aspect of his work cannot be overstated. In fact, Maybeck's architecture frequently resulted specifically from his response to the site, the broader landscape context in which he worked, and a desire to manipulate and to include them as part of his design.

Maybeck's buildings and landscapes must be examined together. The architect's drawings and writings show that much of his architecture, though certainly a product of his proclivity for stylistic borrowing and invention, resulted also from the careful integration of building and landscape. In fact, landscape design was frequently the architect's overriding concern and at times took precedence over the design of buildings.[8] Considering the number of projects Maybeck undertook during his career —over two hundred according to the lists compiled by Cardwell and Woodbridge and confirmed by the Environmental Design Archives' catalog—relatively few include traditional planting plans, nor do many of his technical drawings address landscape design alone. It is perhaps for this reason that many architectural historians have failed to see Maybeck as a landscape designer.[9] Yet the majority of his design drawings and sketches include landscape elements that are an essential aspect of his work.

Maybeck's integration of architecture and landscape places him in the company of many other West Coast architects, including Willis Polk, Louis Christian Mullgardt, Julia Morgan, Irving Gill, the Greene brothers, and Frank Lloyd Wright —recent studies reveal a significant number of early twentieth-century architects from across the United States for whom landscape considerations played a key role.[10] Like his contemporaries, Maybeck frequently collaborated with landscape architects and nurserymen. Still, his work remains noteworthy for its consistent engagement with landscape and for the clever and thoughtful means by which he integrated buildings and gardens, site and structure.

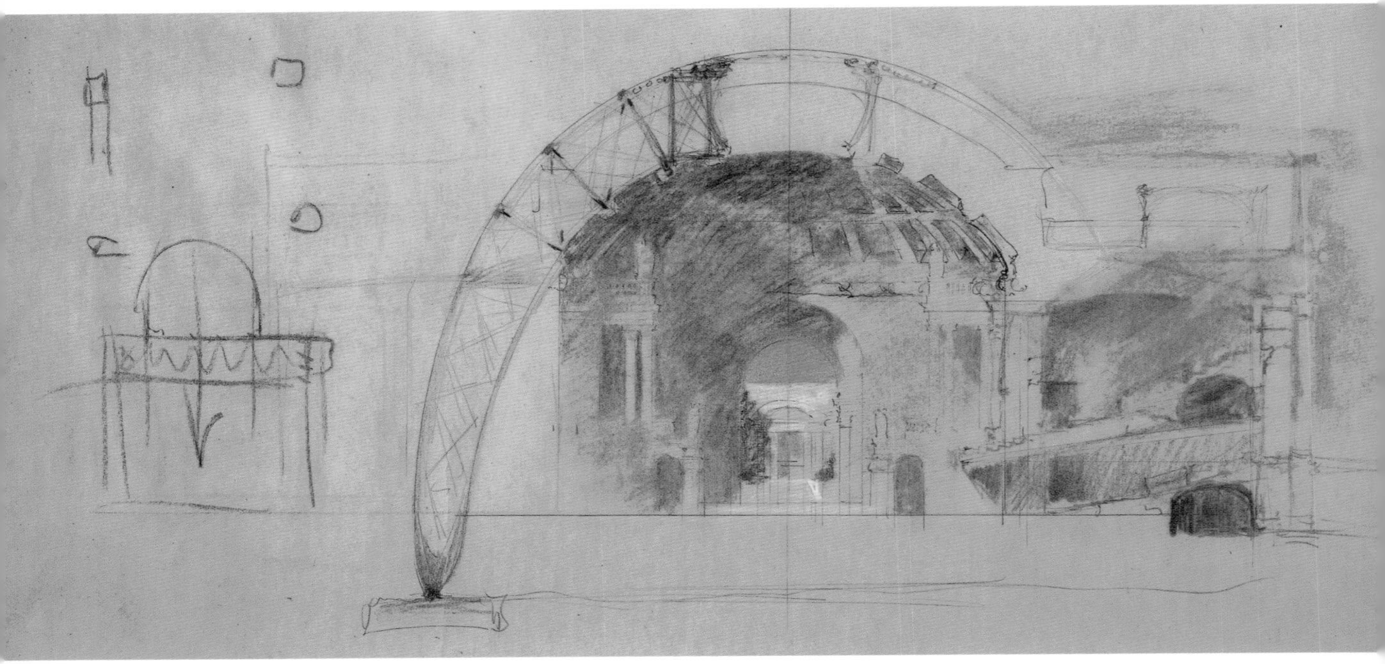

FIGURE 2

PHOEBE HEARST MEMORIAL, UNIVERSITY OF CALIFORNIA, BERKELEY, CIRCA 1922. STUDY.

ARCHITECTURE, ENGINEERING, AND LANDSCAPE ARE IMAGINED SIMULTANEOUSLY IN THIS EARLY STUDY. [EDA, UCB]

A pastel rendering on brown paper made as an early study for the Phoebe Apperson Hearst Memorial on the University of California campus (circa 1922) indicates the architect's design approach perfectly: architecture, structural system, and landscape appear together in a single drawing such that all three are integrated from the earliest phases of design development [figure 2]. For this Hearst Memorial study—typical of Maybeck's work—the structure frames the landscape beyond, capturing and giving it primacy as the central and brightest element on the page. The pervasive appearance of landscape in his drawings—renderings of light (which is essentially a landscape element, though a dynamic and ethereal one), floral and foliate color, water, sky, and the texture and chiaroscuro created by masses of vegetation—indicate the extent of the architect's intense focus on the subject. Examination of Maybeck's choices and placement of plants in relation to his architecture, the formal layout of his grounds, his use of color, and design of water elements reveal specific design strategies that remain consistent despite the wide range in scale, type, and style of design.

The stylistic eclecticism of Maybeck's landscape designs matches that of his architectural works. His gardens borrow forms and images from those of France, Italy, England (especially the English cottage garden), and the imagined landscapes of California's missions among others. Yet beyond this stylistic collage resides a distinctly regional quality derived from a design sensibility that was largely pictorial and romantic, culled from the image of California—both northern and southern—as a Mediterranean paradise, a notion that originated in the mid-1800s. This "Mediterranean analogy," as the California historian Kevin Starr called it, became a rich source of imagery for Maybeck and his contemporaries, and the idea and mythology of a Mediterranean California enjoyed wide currency throughout the nation. Whether viewed as "Roma Pacifica" or as the "Athens of the West," California's climate, agricultural fertility, and apparent abundance provided ample basis for the construction of an identity linked with Greece and Italy.[11]

Maybeck's adherence to this Mediterranean ideal appears in his unpublished 1918 essay on regional architecture, written as he was designing a general ground plan with suggested tree types for the Mills College campus in Oakland. He wrote,

> *Fortunately, Mills College is in California, and the question of snow and ice does not enter, making our problem easier to solve geographically; the fundamental principle will be that which developed in the similar climate of rain and flowers found around the Mediterranean Sea. The style of Mills College should be appropriate to the Oakland climate, and influenced by the fact that vines do not freeze in winter, that Oakland is not the home of coconut trees, that flowering bushes thrive — in fact, that as a first and fixed principle it is a garden spot of the earth, combining the fruit of the North and many Southern fruits.*[12]

What initially reads as an intuitive sensitivity to regional ecology equally expresses the belief—common for the time—that the Bay Area was culturally and climatically an Arcadian land of plenty. In likening the climate of Oakland to that of the Mediterranean, Maybeck joined the vast ranks of Americans who saw the West Coast as a promised land of warmth and bounty. Although the vision has endured, the state's frequent droughts and recurring water shortages underscore the ecological problems inherent to that imagery. If California is an Arcadia, it is an unpredictable one in which metaphoric rivers of milk, honey, and wine may flow, but where actual rivers of water are neither reliable nor abundant.[13] As such, the Californian/Mediterranean fantasy resulted from a combination of booster activities intended to attract population and capital with the West Coast version of American pastoralism. Represented on citrus crate labels, postcards, in the paintings of William Keith and Arthur and Lucia Mathews (discussed below), and as the inspiration for Isadora Duncan's dances, the ideal was just that—fiction more than fact, but a fantasy that found translation in Maybeck's landscapes [figures 3, 4]. His drawings and built works include twisted oaks; sculptures of toga-clad women adorn his planter boxes; Italian cypresses and trellises covered with grapes or wisteria recur; and golden and

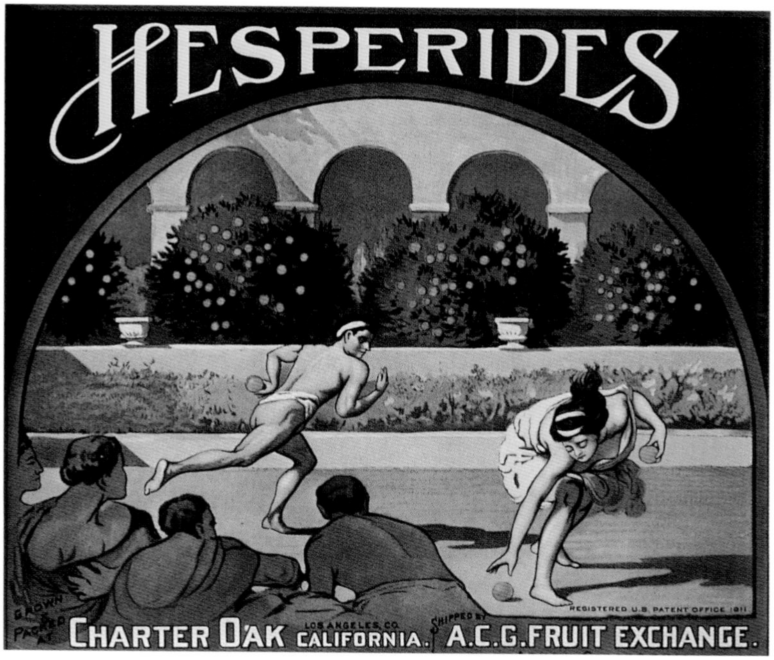

FIGURE 3 *(above)*

ORANGE CRATE LABEL ILLUSTRATING MEDITERRANEAN CALIFORNIA.

[MARC TREIB]

FIGURE 4 *(below)*

ISADORA DUNCAN IN THE THEATRE OF DIONYSUS, ATHENS, 1903.

[RAYMOND DUNCAN, THE BANCROFT LIBRARY, UNIVERSITY OF CALIFORNIA, BERKELEY]

warm tones predominate in his renderings—all combining to create a series of Mediterranean-inspired landscapes [figures 5, 6].

According to Starr, the proliferation of these Mediterranean ideas can be traced to the 1840s and John Charles Fremont. Fremont first arrived in California in the spring of 1844 and by 1845 he had written and published his "Report of the Exploring Expedition to Oregon and Northern California," which made extended comparisons of California with Italy. Starr considers Fremont's text to be "the founding text of the Mediterranean analogy." These comparisons, based on similarities of landscape and climate, became quite compelling, developing over time into "a metaphor for all that California offered as a regional civilization. Suggesting new textures and values of living, California-as-Mediterranean challenged Americans to embrace beauty and to escape the Puritan past." California was still the new frontier, and its inhabitants needed to demonstrate the state's cultural equality with the rest of the country, particularly the East Coast. By comparing California to Italy and Greece, countries embodying the cultural achievements of the classical past, Fremont—and Maybeck fifty years later—claimed some of that cultural importance for themselves. So committed was Fremont to this Californian/Italian imagery, that he created an Italianate estate for himself in Mariposa, located in California's gold country foothills, complete with Native American servants dressed as Italian peasants. He modeled his home after an Italian villa and employed Frederick Law Olmsted to advise on his landscape design, resulting in a house that prefigured Bay Region architecture in its strong connection to the site and use of exposed wood.[14] Although never constructed, Olmsted's plan for his own home at the Mariposa mining estate included "deep piazzas or galleries with low shades" to allow for cooling ventilation, for a "rough-hewn character in outline and detail" to fit with the landscape, and for the use of wood, which was plentiful and could provide "admirable lights and shadows." He wanted a "chalet" that looked as though it was "knocked up by some mountaineer with a genius."[15]

Olmsted too saw Mediterranean overtones in California's landscape, describing the scenery near Bear Valley as similar to that seen in Italy. His San Francisco Bay Area projects of the mid-1860s sought an appropriate response that embraced the semi-arid environment, and he therefore recalled memories of Italian villas he had visited during a European tour. Although Olmsted helped establish the irregular/picturesque landscape in the Bay Area with his 1865 Mountain View Cemetery in Oakland, his Stanford campus plan of 1888 with its mission-inspired courtyard arrangements resonated with the common understanding of the state's heritage. With that plan, Olmsted may have been among the earliest designers to establish the idea that appropriate design for California included a thorough blending of indoors and out.[16]

Despite the high praise for the state's natural setting, and the widely accepted notion of its Arcadian abundance, designers and reformers believed the landscape required improving to reach its full aesthetic and/or productive potential. If California was a land of plenitude and luxuriance, it was one that had to be cultivated, ordered, and brought into focus by creating gardens, both public and private. Maybeck, with others of his generation, inherited these attitudes and values. But he also brought a French design education to his Californian work that, when combined with the influence of a circle of Bay Area cultural elites, resulted in his distinctive form of practice.

FIGURE 5

PLANTER BOXES AT THE HEARST MEMORIAL GYMNASIUM, UNIVERSITY OF CALIFORNIA, BERKELEY, 1925.

[DIANNE HARRIS]

FIGURE 6 *(opposite)*

WESTERN HILLS CEMETERY, LAWNDALE, 1940. BERNARD MAYBECK AND JULIA MORGAN. DRAWING.

[EDA, UCB]

EDUCATION AND PARALLELS

Maybeck studied at the École des Beaux-Arts in Paris from 1882 to 1886—there his formal architectural training began. During that period Julien Guadet lectured on architectural theory, providing Maybeck with a fundamental understanding of principles related to architectural order and form, based on Guadet's study and interpretation of the classical past.[17] Outside the school, Gottfried Semper's and Owen Jones's theories on architectural polychromy rose in popularity. Though Semper and Jones exercised little direct influence on education at the École, their published work from the period, as Kenneth Cardwell has noted, influenced Maybeck's professional development.[18] From their work he undoubtedly learned about many aspects of architectural design, but their ideas about the application of color to a building and its relation to the surrounding environment were particularly important for the formulation of Maybeck's landscape sensibility.

Design projects at the École des Beaux-Arts included some of the building types Maybeck produced during his career. In the last decades of the nineteenth century, popular subjects for competitions and study at the École included public baths, monuments, schools, and various public buildings.[19] International exhibition buildings were likewise favored, so it is not surprising that during the early years of his career Maybeck had such confidence and success designing structures for the Panama Pacific International Exposition (which opened in 1915). As Annie Jacques has noted, town planning was virtually ignored at the school, and Maybeck more likely derived his knowledge of urban design and planning from personal observation and reading. École faculty like Guadet and his predecessor, Guillaume, placed little emphasis on innovation or exploration of contemporary themes, preferring instead to teach from a fairly stock set of nineteenth-century design problems.[20] Like most architects of his generation therefore, Maybeck never fully embraced the stylistic tenets of European or international-style modernism when it emerged, preferring for most of his career to manipulate the traditions of the past (though frequently experimenting with new or unusual materials), reinterpreting them for contemporary social and environmental conditions. Thus neither Maybeck's work nor that of his contemporaries should be evaluated against a proto-modernist yardstick but should instead be judged on its own terms.

Little precise information records landscape-related pedagogy at the École at the end of the nineteenth century, although student renderings frequently displayed elaborate landscapes surrounding their architectural designs and sometimes even included rooftop planting. A similar elaboration of landscape appears in the École drawings of Jules-Léon Chifflot, whose 1903 restoration for the House of the Centenarian at Pompeii illustrated gardens inside, outside, and behind the house, and of the Californian architect Warren Perry, whose "Orangerie" (circa 1908–11) depicted extensive rooftop and terrace vegetation [figure 7].[21]

While in Paris, Maybeck studied in the atelier of Louis-Jules André who, according to Kenneth Cardwell, had a strong feeling for natural forms and advocated the design of landscape to strengthen and unify his compositions.[22] André's absorbing work from 1872–85, the period of Maybeck's tenure at the École, was "the design of grounds and buildings for one of France's largest public gardens, the Jardin des Plantes." It is therefore probable that Maybeck first became interested in the design of landscape and the relation of building and environment through André. So great must André's emphasis on landscape design have been that a Hillside Club yearbook for 1906–07 referred to him as "the great Landscape Architect," rather than as the architect he primarily was.[23]

Moreover, Maybeck had experienced the streets, squares, and parks of late nineteenth-century Paris during his student years. The parks he encountered were largely the work of Second Empire designers and in the *style paysager*, composed primarily

FIGURE 7

"ORANGERIE," CIRCA 1908–11. WARREN PERRY.
STUDENT DRAWING FROM THE
ÉCOLE DES BEAUX-ARTS, PARIS.
[THE BANCROFT LIBRARY,
UNIVERSITY OF CALIFORNIA, BERKELEY]

FIGURE 8

VESTIBULE OF THE BIBLIOTHÈQUE STE-GENEVIÈVE, PARIS, 1850. HENRI LABROUSTE.

NOTE THE VEGETATION PAINTED ON THE INTERIOR WALLS.

[DAVID HAYS]

of so-called picturesque or irregular landscape forms that were not geometrically ordered. According to Dorothée Imbert, turn-of-the-century Paris witnessed a series of fluctuations in landscape theory that "oscillated between the two extremes" of irregular Virgilian pastoralism and severe geometry.[24] Édouard André's 1879 treatise, which advocated a *style composite* using a combination of naturalistic and formal manners, was a major source on landscape design that Maybeck might have encountered.[25] At the turn of the twentieth century, the influence of Achille Duchêne's reintroduction of historicist parterres and geometric formality prevailed alongside the irregular models of previous decades, such that Maybeck's early exposure to landscape design included an eclectic array of styles that ranged from the *paysager* to the *régulier*, thereby matching his architectural proclivity for eclecticism.[26]

In addition to the influence of both Louis-Jules and Édouard André and the object lessons of the late Second Empire Parisian landscape, most of the design problems assigned to Maybeck and his fellow students at the École were large, urban projects, which by their very nature forced students to address the surrounding context. A review of student projects indicates that École tradition included romanticizing architecture through the extensive use of landscape, especially through the use of water.[27] Yet this romantic use of landscape had not always been looked upon favorably by the École academicians.

For example, Henri Labrouste's Bibliothèque Ste-Geneviève of 1850 was decorated to resemble an "illusionistic garden" with its murals of trees and trellislike ironwork [figure 8]. Its conception as an outdoor reading place that would have "the advantage of offering trees always green and always in bloom... without regard for the climate of Paris," caused some contemporary critics to find it too romantic.[28] However, as an example known to Maybeck, this building might have provided an important precedent with its vestibule's indoor-outdoor quality that served as both a liminal transition zone from the street and an illusionistic Platonic grove, complete with a ceiling once painted to resemble a blue sky, trees whose branches hovered above the sculpted heads of French luminaries, and green iron structural supports.[29] The use of landscape to evoke moods was part of a trend—visible in numerous student drawings—that surfaced at the École sometime during the mid-1800s as a form of the Néo-Grec, itself a Romantic movement.[30]

Moreover, in the 1870s student projects began to appear with landscape design as their primary subjects, such as Émile Bénard's 1871 reconstruction of the gardens at the Villa Madama in Rome.[31] This project and others like it reflected the priorities of the academy, accepting landscape design and reconstruction as legitimate subjects for study, and serving at least in part to explain the source of Maybeck's interest in and knowledge of landscape. Typical of Beaux-Arts designers of his time, Maybeck frequently used elaborate water schemes in his public projects and always strove to evoke romantic atmospheres in this École tradition.

Apart from formal education, learned men and women of the late nineteenth century commonly educated themselves about nature and the surrounding landscape. For example, Joseph LeConte, who arrived in California in 1869 and became professor of geology and natural history at the University of California, Berkeley, helped define "California academic style as a blend of serious thinking and passionate outdoorsmanship."[32] Many cultured individuals of the period explored literature, science, and the arts, but they also had a naturalist's understanding of the landscape.

Although no evidence exists regarding the contents of his personal library, Maybeck was both a serious thinker and a passionate outdoorsman who undoubtedly taught himself a great deal about plants and their appropriate use and arrangement by reading a range of publications. Like the landscapes he observed in Paris, the prevailing European and North American design trends were eclectic, either combining or oscillating between geometrically formal and/or naturalistic or irregular forms. From the 1880s through the 1930s, the well-known (and initially literary) debate raged in England between the classically formal prescriptions of the architects Reginald Blomfield and John Sedding, and the diametrically opposed English cottage garden that inspired landscape designers William Robinson and later Gertrude Jekyll, the primary proponents of the "wild garden" in late nineteenth-century England.[33] Blomfield believed that gardens should be laid out in accordance with the architectural lines of the house's plan, and his book, *The Formal Garden in England* (1892), included numerous illustrations of carefully composed gardens with terraces, clipped hedges, regular pools of water, and even topiary [figure 9]. Robinson, author of numerous books including *The Wild Garden* (1870), advocated a garden that embraced the properties of the picturesque or irregular style but were created at the reduced scale more common to the estates of Britain's late nineteenth-century upper crust.[34] Avid horticulturalists, they likewise advocated the use of wildflowers and common English native plants, massed as carefully composed beds

FIGURE 9

GARDEN AND TERRACE: MONTACUTE.
[REGINALD BLOMFIELD AND INIGO THOMAS, *THE FORMAL GARDEN IN ENGLAND* (1892)]

of texture and color in herbaceous borders [figure 10]. Although the idea of the herbaceous perennial border appeared around 1830, Gertrude Jekyll popularized it in a more subtle form by 1900, emphasizing as her guiding principles the properties of the individual plant, proper blending of color, and the display of color for as long as possible. Both Jekyll and Robinson wrote profusely on gardening and their books were widely read from 1880 to 1935, the period coinciding with the height of Maybeck's career.

Interpretations and critiques of Blomfield's and Sedding's writings appeared in the United States by the 1890s. Charles Platt, Wilson Eyre, and Frank Miles Day (the two latter founded *House and Garden* in 1901) similarly advocated formal, geometric approaches to landscape and garden design, but they tended to mass plants informally within their geometric schemes. Moreover, the northern Californian Bruce Porter's landscape designs were geometrically disposed and organized along grand axes.[35]

FIGURE 10

FRONTISPIECE. ALFRED PARSONS, ARTIST

[WILLIAM ROBINSON,
THE WILD GARDEN, 1870]

Yet the Robinson-Jekyll tradition appeared on American soil as well, introduced in the first decades of the century through Jekyll's publications and through the works of practitioners such as Beatrix Jones Farrand, who combined the looser style of the herbaceous border within classically designed gardens.[36] For the first three or four decades of the century, schools of landscape architecture in the United States generally instructed their students in Beaux-Arts classicism, teaching a style that translated into the country estates and civic spaces clients then demanded. In fact, from 1890 until 1940, estate design in the United States largely followed that model: formally arranged grounds within which flowers appeared in informal masses.[37]

Maybeck shared Jekyll and Robinson's ideas about garden color, particularly in striving for extended blooming periods. Indeed, Maybeck's renderings often included flower borders that are "Jekyll-esque" in character. But the architect's eclectic embrace of both geometrical forms and the irregular style was typical for his time. Although completed late in his career, Maybeck's designs for Principia College in Elsah, Illinois (1930–38), indicate his interest in this British precedent. The landscape design for the campus mixes picturesque campus planning with English cottage garden imagery. In an early letter to the Principia founders, Maybeck wrote that he was striving for a "picturesque setting" with buildings arranged like cottages "in a low English wall." A magazine clipping among Maybeck's papers illustrates an English cottage garden and exemplifies the imagery that served as a model for the plan [figure 11].[38]

Aside from the English overlay, the most significant aspect of the Principia plan was its initial conception, in which site planning and design were based on the unique features of the southern Illinois landscape. Based on research undertaken before his first journey to the campus site, Maybeck produced a sketch indicating the most prominent features of the Missouri / Illinois landscape: the Mississippi River, the bluffs, and the floodplain. The architect wrote,

FIGURE 11

CLIPPING FOUND IN MAYBECK'S FILES FOR THE PRINCIPIA COLLEGE PROJECT.

THE IMAGE INDICATES MAYBECK'S AFFECTION FOR THE ENGLISH COTTAGE GARDEN.

[EDA, UCB]

> *The best feature of your landscape in the St. Louis area is rivers. We'll find a property on a river. We want high ground, and so we'll locate the property on bluffs about your river, and on the highest point, we'll place the chapel. We'll want a long row of trees leading into the center of the property. Lots of trees all about the place, and land that falls into interesting contours.*[39]

Sensitivity to region and the inherent attributes of a place, then, were not restricted to Maybeck's work in California, nor was his concern for landscape and planting. The campus was indeed located on the river bluffs and the plan laid out according to topography and positions of existing trees. On the campus's planting Maybeck wrote, "Our responsibility to the future is the planting of the setting...so that they will have a completed garden with their new buildings. Therefore at the earliest moment trees and shrubs might be planted."[40] Although the Principia architecture may not be his best, the campus plan indicates Maybeck's interest in the design of the landscape developed from the project's inception and in tandem with the architecture and general campus plan.

In California the main thrust of turn-of-the-century garden theory was "a desire to strike a balance between variety and design, indulgence and restraint...the control of lushness through design—constraint, simplicity and order."[41] Gardens focused the state's bounty, but in such a way that this luxury might be easily read, its qualities magnified and controlled for ease of perception. Moreover, the integration of house and garden increased in popularity after the mid-1800s. But by the early 1900s, magazines such as *House and Garden* and *The Craftsman* popularized the idea with frequently featured articles on gardens designed as an extension of the domestic architecture, advancing the notion that California's distinctive climate necessitated an indoor-outdoor lifestyle that implied a merging of building and landscape. A 1908 *Craftsman* article stated,

> *Climatically and geographically, conditions on the Pacific Coast are exceptionally favorable for the development of a distinctly local style in the building*

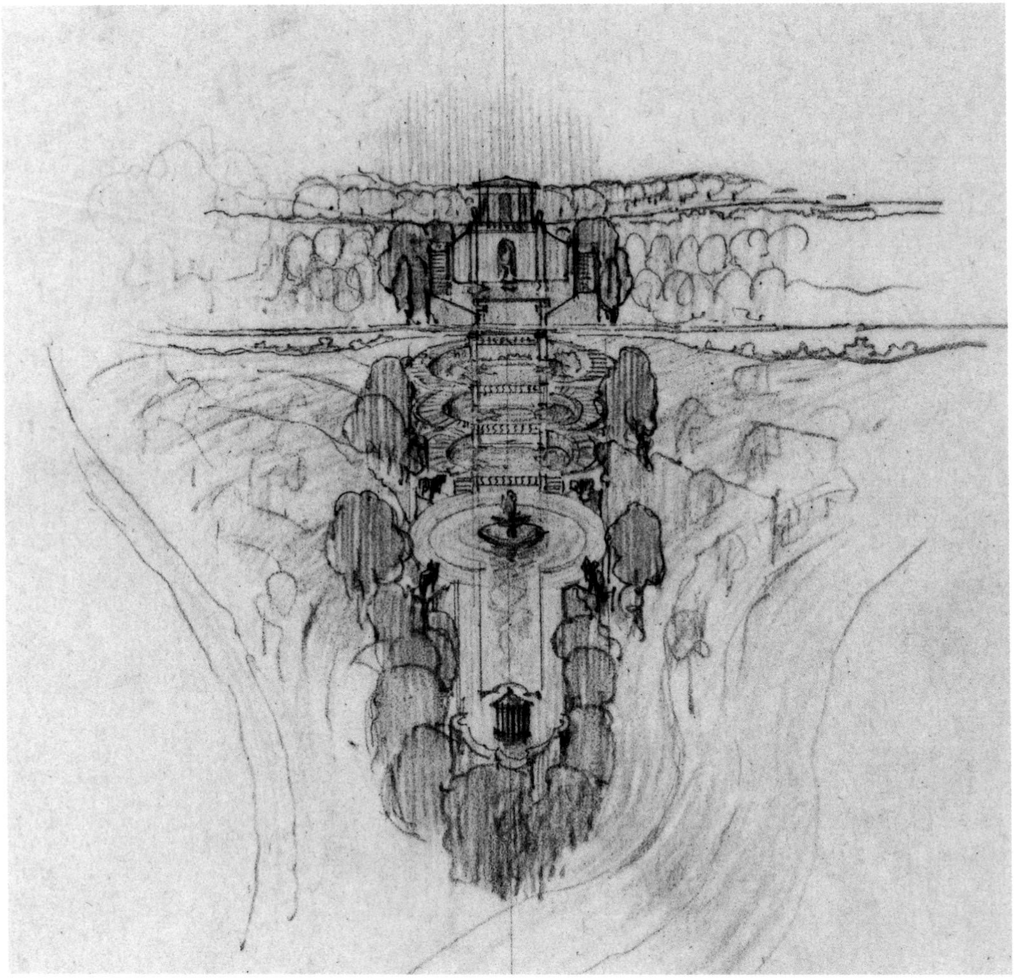

FIGURE 12

HEARST CASTLE, SAN SIMEON, 1925–29.
JULIA MORGAN.
STUDY FOR FEATURE ADJOINING SWIMMING POOL.
[EDA, UCB]

> *art. Because of its climatic conditions, the possibilities for attractive outdoor effects such as pergolas, courtyards, terraces and gardens, which should always be included in the general architectural scheme, are almost unlimited.*[42]

Such descriptions, in addition to a range of articles that appeared in popular and professional magazines, inspired architects throughout the state and in other parts of the country to fashion houses intimately linked with gardens.[43]

As an active member of the architectural profession in California, Maybeck participated in a culture that included Irving Gill, Charles and Henry Greene, as well as the prominent Bay Area practitioners such as Willis Polk, Louis Christian Mullgardt, Ernest Coxhead, Julia Morgan, and A. C. Schweinfurth. All these architects were actively engaged with landscape design to some extent — again, the shortage of local practitioners at that time meant that most architects had at least to dabble in designing outdoor spaces. Nearly all forged strong relationships with those landscape architects and nurserymen who were available; Gill worked closely with Kate Sessions in southern California. At times Morgan collaborated with Charles Gibbs Adams when not designing her own landscapes [figure 12].[44] Maybeck joined forces with various designers throughout his career including Butler Sturtevant, John McLaren, George Hansen, John Gregg, and Mark Daniels.[45] Although they contributed significantly to the field of landscape architecture in California, little scholarship has yet elucidated the careers of these men and women.

As the architectural historian Esther McCoy noted, Gill was partial to "the dark glossy greens of pittosporums and the *Coprosma baueri* used as screens, or as cool depths to look into from porch or terrace. The trim on his houses was invariably dark green, borrowed from his plantings. One of his favorite effects came from massing red geraniums near the house." Gill believed that the house should be plain and simple, ornamented by nature, "who will tone it with lichens, chisel it with storms, make it gracious and friendly with vines and flower shadows as she

FIGURE 13 *(above)*

WOMEN'S CLUB, LA JOLLA, 1913. IRVING GILL.

[MARC TREIB]

FIGURE 14 *(below)*

GAMBLE HOUSE, PASADENA, 1908.
GREENE AND GREENE.

[MARC TREIB]

does the stone in the meadow."[46] A house "unornamented save for the vines that soften a line or creepers that wreathe a pillar," Gill argued, "or flowers that inlay color more sentiently than any tile could do" added enormously to the design of dwellings.[47] Landscape then, was the only ornamentation Gill allowed on his spare buildings and he used concrete stepping-stone blocks to carry the architectonic qualities of the house into the garden. As Gill did, Maybeck would encourage the growth of vines to carry the garden onto the walls of the house [figure 13].

The architects Charles and Henry Greene similarly used planter boxes to bring vegetation onto the house, as at the Gamble house in Pasadena where they designed the planter boxes as part of the railing detail for the sleeping porches [figure 14]. In their 1907 Blacker house, the floral-pattern stained-glass windows of the stairway "echoed the flowers incorporated in the design of the planting scheme for the garden outside the window."[48]

The work of any number of architects might have influenced Maybeck, but Frank Lloyd Wright's forms an obvious point of comparison. Wright's renderings, like Maybeck's, frequently contain intriguing landscape elaborations, and he collaborated on their designs with Jens Jensen and Walter Burley Griffin. Wright scholars note the importance of site features in determining the organization of his designs, and there is little doubt that his oeuvre involved a complex understanding of, and intense interest in, landscape design.[49] Although an in-depth analysis of Wright's landscape sensibility lies outside the scope of this book, a generalized comparison reveals that Wright's schemes extended the lines of his architecture into the landscape; in contrast, Maybeck drew the landscape into his architecture. Of course, Wright's stained glass and decorative motifs based on abstractions of regional or local landscape features and vegetation are a striking exception to this statement. And as Anne Spirn has noted, Wright (like Maybeck) "shaped landscapes as scenes framed by windows and designed buildings to be seen as part of a landscape," and he created explicit correspondences between "framed views of the landscape outside a building" and paintings of landscapes on the walls within. As Maybeck did, Wright read and admired Jekyll's work, as seen in his Taliesin plantings that resemble Jekyll's flower borders. Yet Wright adhered more consistently than Maybeck to landscape compositions that were regulated by orthogonal grids derived from either the building or the site context, and he more consistently favored the use of native plant species and retention of an apparently "natural" setting for his buildings [figure 15].[50] However important Wright may seem as a source today, Maybeck seldom referred overtly to Wright's work, although he was certainly aware of it.[51] Wright has become a major touchstone for most historians and critics of American architecture, but he was not necessarily so for all the architects of his generation. Still, as Spirn asserted, "Wright's work is part of a larger tradition of architecture that embraces the idea of landscape and building as continuous," and it is within this context that we should consider both architect's careers.[52]

It is more clear, however, that direct contact with Polk, Mullgardt, Coxhead, and Schweinfurth certainly had an impact on Maybeck. These architects started their practices in California a decade before Maybeck — Polk and Schweinfurth both worked in the office of A. Page Brown, where Maybeck found early employment as a draftsman. Coxhead and Polk embraced Arts and Crafts ideas and, like their Bay Area neighbors, deeply admired the local landscape. Polk's designs demonstrated what Richard Longstreth has called "a spirited accommodation" to the topography of San Francisco, marking "a new attitude toward the landscape that would have a far-reaching impact on the area's residential architecture in succeeding decades," and his designs for San Francisco's Russian Hill included a series of Italianate terraces with heavy planting, indicating a similar interest in landscape as an integrated part of design endeavors. Although Polk also embraced the English vernacular architecture then popular with Arts and Crafts designers, his landscapes nonetheless adhered to classical European models. His 1897–98 Empire Cottage design for William Bourn's

FIGURE 15

BARNSDALL [HOLLYHOCK] HOUSE, LOS ANGELES, 1917+. FRANK LLOYD WRIGHT. GARDEN VIEW.

NOTE THE ABSTRACT CONCRETE HOLLYHOCKS AND EXTENSION OF THE BUILDING'S LINES INTO THE LANDSCAPES
[MARC TREIB]

cottage in the Sierra foothills incorporated an elaborately terraced garden with a cascade that emptied into a rectangular basin and clipped vines and hedges that emphasized the geometric lines of the garden's paths and walls. Likewise, Polk's garden design for Beaulieu, the Cupertino estate of Charles Baldwin (1900–01), included a geometrically formal garden based on classical models from France and Italy [figure 16]. However, Polk helped establish eclecticism in the region by combining these forms with vegetation that, if not native, was at least strongly associated with the Californian landscape: palm trees, live oaks, eucalyptus, and so on.[53] Like other designers at this time, Polk frequently collaborated with landscape architects —Bruce Porter (an interior designer who also created the Filoli gardens for the Bourn estate in Woodside) worked with him on the Carolans in Burlingame Park (1899). Moreover, Mullgardt's 1908 competition entry for a house intended to cost under $3,000 indicated a strong feeling for classical landscape design. Named The Poplars, Mullgardt's design included geometrically defined areas of lawn, a pergola-covered walkway, parterre-like terraces, and a large vegetable garden. Planter boxes placed under all the windows and vines planted at the foundation allowed vegetation to cover a substantial portion of the facade.[54]

Maybeck's garden plan for the Leon Roos house, designed in 1909 for a prominent San Francisco family, indicates that he too sometimes subscribed to the classical model of residential design and the scheme follows many of the same principles as Mullgardt's coeval competition entry. The Roos house exemplifies the "total design" advocated by the Arts and Crafts movement and is also one of Maybeck's most well known residential commissions. He designed furnishings and light fixtures for the house and a family crest that appears as a motif in many of the details [figure 17]. He also designed the front garden and a rear parcel that included an elaborate formal vegetable garden on an adjacent lot once considered part of the family's property. When the family sold the property, now occupied by large residences, the rear garden was destroyed. However, the garden plan remains for study, drawn in Maybeck's hand

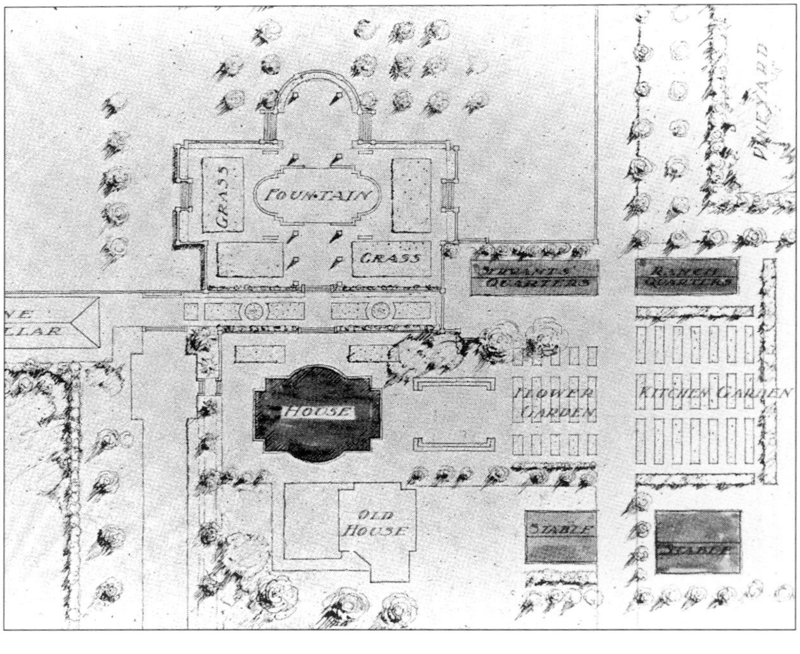

FIGURE 16

BEAULIEU, CUPERTINO, 1900–1901. WILLIS POLK.
GARDEN PLAN.

[*HOUSE AND GARDEN*, DECEMBER 1902]

FIGURE 17

LEON ROOS RESIDENCE, SAN FRANCISCO, 1909.
DRAWING FOR EAST ELEVATION.
[EDA, UCB]

at 1/4″ scale, in addition to some photos of the garden, that record the realization of the architect's design [figures 18, 19].

The scheme's geometry determined a symmetrical series of orthogonal, interconnecting flagstone and gravel paths that converged at the center of the garden. A central water basin served as the focal point of the space, and a wall enclosed the entirety. The plan depicts the massing of plant materials as well as the intended type, although not specific species. Maybeck specified the groupings of plants, keeping the lower vegetable beds in the center of the garden around the water basin, and massing plants according to their height, moving higher toward the outer edges, with "permanent hedges" giving way to "high bushes and fruit trees" followed by "vines and wall fruit" against the enclosing walls. He therefore created a garden carefully sheltered from the wind, an important consideration on the hilltop site. Thus the geometrically disposed garden with its extensive vegetable plot closely resembles Mullgardt's competition entry, but adapted to fit Maybeck's client and site.

In addition to Mullgardt, Polk, and the other architects working in the Bay Area, Maybeck also profited from contact with some of the influential artists and intellectuals who dominated the local scene at the turn of the century.[55] The Berkeley poet Charles Keeler—who became Maybeck's first residential client—joined forces with the architect to become "the most vocal proponents of an indigenous Arts and Crafts movement in Berkeley." Primarily a journalist, Keeler became interested in residential design while constructing his own home in the Berkeley hills, and he dedicated his book *The Simple Home* (1904) to his "friend and Counselor Bernard R. Maybeck." Both men possessed an amateur's understanding of nature and horticulture; thus the book likely represents what Keeler learned from Maybeck. *The Simple Home* suggested that the entirety of the physical environment should become a work of art, and an entire chapter concerns guidelines for designing residential gardens, including lists of plants deemed appropriate for use in a variety of conditions.[56]

For a "natural" garden in California's coastal zone, Keeler listed "redwoods, live oaks, madrones, manzanitas, wild currants, red buds, azaleas" as appropriate along with a variety of wildflowers. He further recommended the introduction of exotic plants into the natural garden because he believed a garden of exclusively indigenous species would be "too colorless." Keeler's admiration for the Californian climate that "allows plants to thrive which elsewhere must be grown under glass," fostered his enthusiasm for exotic plants.[57] He therefore endorsed bamboo, palms, dracaenas, magnolias, oranges, bananas, eucalyptus, acacias, pittosporums, grevilleas, and auracarias. Most important, Keeler wrote, was to "strive for a mass of bloom at all periods of the year," and he provided a sample blooming cycle in which iris give way to tulips and cannas, leading to poppies, hollyhocks and sweet peas in summer, followed by chrysanthemums in autumn. He recommended geraniums and roses because they bloom almost year-round in the Californian climate. Whether these ideas originated with Keeler or with Maybeck, they accurately depict the architect's approach to planting design.

In addition to listing suitable plants for gardens in northern California, Keeler proposed a range of styles he deemed appropriate for a simple home garden in the North Berkeley hills. He defined two types of garden—again, typical for the times—the "natural" and the "formal," noting that these types were distinguished not only in their layout, but also by their vegetation. A "natural" garden was "one that simulates, as nearly as may be, the charm of the wilderness, tamed and diversified for convenience and accessibility." For Keeler, the eighteenth-century English parks exemplified this "natural" garden—the same landscapes Maybeck would have encountered in Paris as the *style paysager*—comprised primarily of what he believed were indigenous plantings. Keeler, like Willis Polk and others, based his "formal garden"—correlating with the French *style régulier*—on Italian models, a formula "arranged according to an architectural plan, with terraces, pools, fountains and watercourses, outdoor rooms, and some suggestions of architectural or sculptural

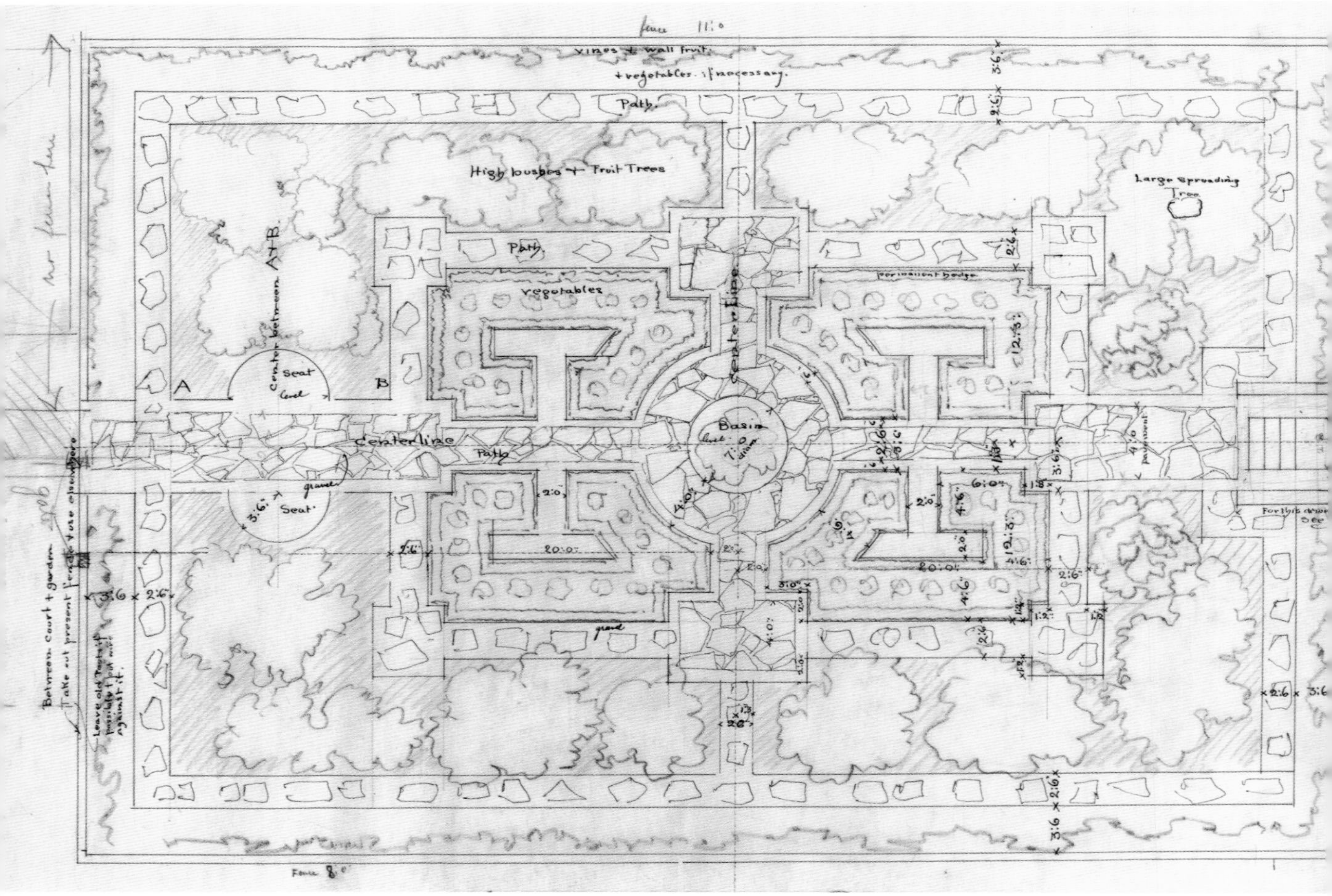

FIGURE 18

LEON ROOS RESIDENCE, SAN FRANCISCO, 1909. PLAN OF VEGETABLE GARDEN.

[EDA, UCB]

FIGURE 19

VEGETABLE GARDEN AT THE REAR OF THE ROOS RESIDENCE, SAN FRANCISCO, CIRCA 1910–15 (DESTROYED).

[EDA, UCB]

adornment."[58] He recommended that the formal garden include both exotic and native plants, seeing the use of natives alone as (again) too restrictive. Though Keeler was an ardent environmentalist, his understanding of the regional ecology leaned more in the direction of bounty than want, and his sense of the virtues of native plants had more to do with artistic preference than an understanding of the need for drought-tolerant species in the unpredictable climate of northern California.

In addition, Keeler recommended study of the Japanese garden, though he pronounced it "too conservative and conventional for the western mind," admiring, however, its "grace and subtlety of finish."[59] He was particularly fond of both the Japanese and Italian use of outdoor rooms and artificial watercourses. In the end, Keeler recommended a compromise between the natural and formal types, which would have appealed to Maybeck's enthusiasm for borrowed and artfully combined styles. Despite the oscillation between formal preferences, Maybeck reinterpreted the traditions of the past to create Californian gardens that were unique in acknowledging the qualities of each site and in their integral relation to architecture.

Together, Maybeck and Keeler provided ideas and examples for a model community in the North Berkeley hills—concepts that were enthusiastically embraced by their neighbors. *The Simple Home* became an important guide for the recently formed Hillside Club, an organization dedicated to the protection of the Berkeley hills. Formed in 1898 by a group of concerned women—with Maybeck's wife, Annie, as one of the founding members—the Hillside Club's objectives were to interest people in building "low houses and broad lanais with plenty of yard room; trying to get people out of doors, interested in flowers and trees and gardens."[60] Maybeck wrote a portion of the club's charter, citing the importance of roadways following the contours of the land, minimal site disturbance, and "house design sympathetic to wooded hillsides left in a near natural state."[61]

Moreover, Werner Hegemann's 1915 Oakland-Berkeley planning report advocated the creation of public and private gardens throughout the city, asserting that gardens were a "great factor in making a city healthy and beautiful," and he lauded Maybeck "for shaping the artistic appearance of the East Bay garden cities."[62] Indeed, Maybeck's design for Berkeley's Rose Walk and his town plans for Brookings, Oregon, demonstrate his interest in creating urban spaces graciously integrated with landscapes. With Rose Walk, Maybeck provided a public garden, connecting hillside neighborhoods to public transit routes along a major street [figure 20].

Rose Walk, from 1912, was one of Maybeck's most significant contributions toward the ideal of Berkeley as a garden city (to adapt Hegemann's term). Designed as one of the public gardens advocated by the Hillside Club, the walk serves as an example of what Frederick Law Olmsted, in his 1865 Berkeley Plan, termed "good outgoings ... requisites of an active neighborhood."[63] The concept for Rose Walk—gardens cascading down a hillside as a spatial link—recurs in Maybeck's designs throughout his career. It appeared in an early generic sketch for a hillside house (circa 1900), in which a series of steps descend a hillside, the landscape passing through the house connecting two levels of the site [figure 21]. The designs for Twin Peaks (examined below) and Western Hills Cemetery likewise share this formal pattern, although neither was intended to function as an urban link. Rose Walk is simultaneously a landmark and a discovered secret, a place where public and private space merge. The arrangement is unconventional since the path allows the public to walk through space that appears to be the private domain of the adjacent homeowners. Their front doors are just a few yards from the sidewalk and from the benches that invite pedestrians to linger in what appear to be private gardens. However, foot traffic remains light, and the design is therefore acceptable to homeowners and the public alike.

FIGURE 20

ROSE WALK, BERKELEY, 1912.

[DIANNE HARRIS]

FIGURE 21

A HILLSIDE HOUSE, CIRCA 1900. SKETCH.

[EDA, UCB]

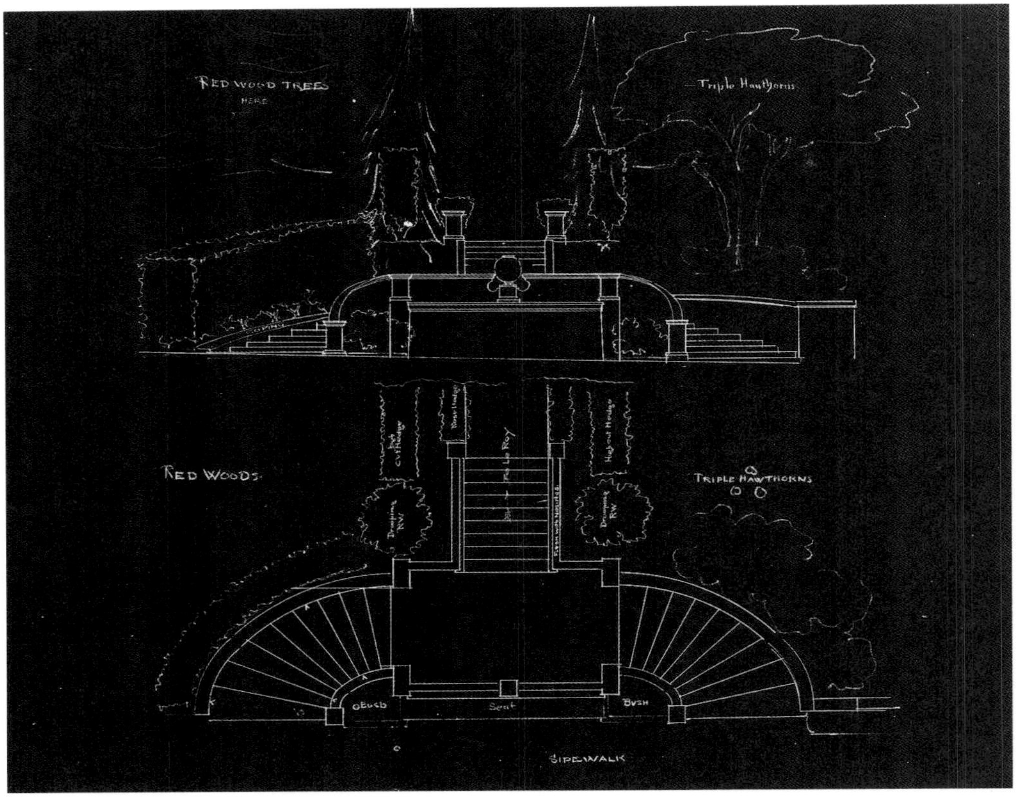

FIGURE 22

ROSE WALK, BERKELEY, 1912.
PLANTING DESIGN.
[THE BANCROFT LIBRARY,
UNIVERSITY OF CALIFORNIA, BERKELEY]

The Italianate design of the path, with the walls, stairs, benches, and planting, illustrate Maybeck's borrowing of Mediterranean forms to allude to a classical past. The pink sidewalk and concrete wall indicate the architect's general predilection for landscape schemes tinted in shades of pink. The planting design for the path called for tall hedges on the southern side of the walk to reinforce the stronger edge created by the houses nearest the pavement [figures 22, 23]. A lower "hedge" (actually more a row) of roses still bloom on the more open, northern side of the path. However, Maybeck's drawings show that he intended a more formal planting scheme than the one seen today. Redwoods placed symmetrically on either side of the walkway near the Euclid Street entrance would have appeared again at the halfway point. Though these do not exist, two very large redwoods planted symmetrically across the path farther to the east provide essentially the same effect Maybeck had indicated in the drawing. The multi-trunked hawthorn shown on the plan is not found anywhere along the walk, although it may have existed at one time, contributing seasonally to the pink color scheme established by the walls and sidewalks.

Rose Walk exemplifies Maybeck's exhortation that neighborhood terraces be "planted systematically in blocks instead of lot — not fifty feet of pink geraniums, twenty-five of nasturtiums, fifty of purple verbena, but long restful lines, big quiet masses."[64] The path remains the architect's strongest contribution toward this ideal and to the making of a city beautiful in Berkeley.

The 1914 Brookings town plan (largely unrealized) contained a central green civic space surrounded by concentric circles of garden housing clusters with courtyards. A drawing included with the Brookings plans shows the architect's intention to camouflage the telegraph and utility poles with vines or other plantings. Maybeck specified "hardy vines" and "vertical pine trees" to hide the poles, and the wires were to be hidden in wooden conduit. Seeing the telegraph pole as a "temporary expedient," Maybeck hoped to reduce their visual impact on the town's surroundings

FIGURE 23

ROSE WALK, BERKELEY, 1912.

[MARC TREIB]

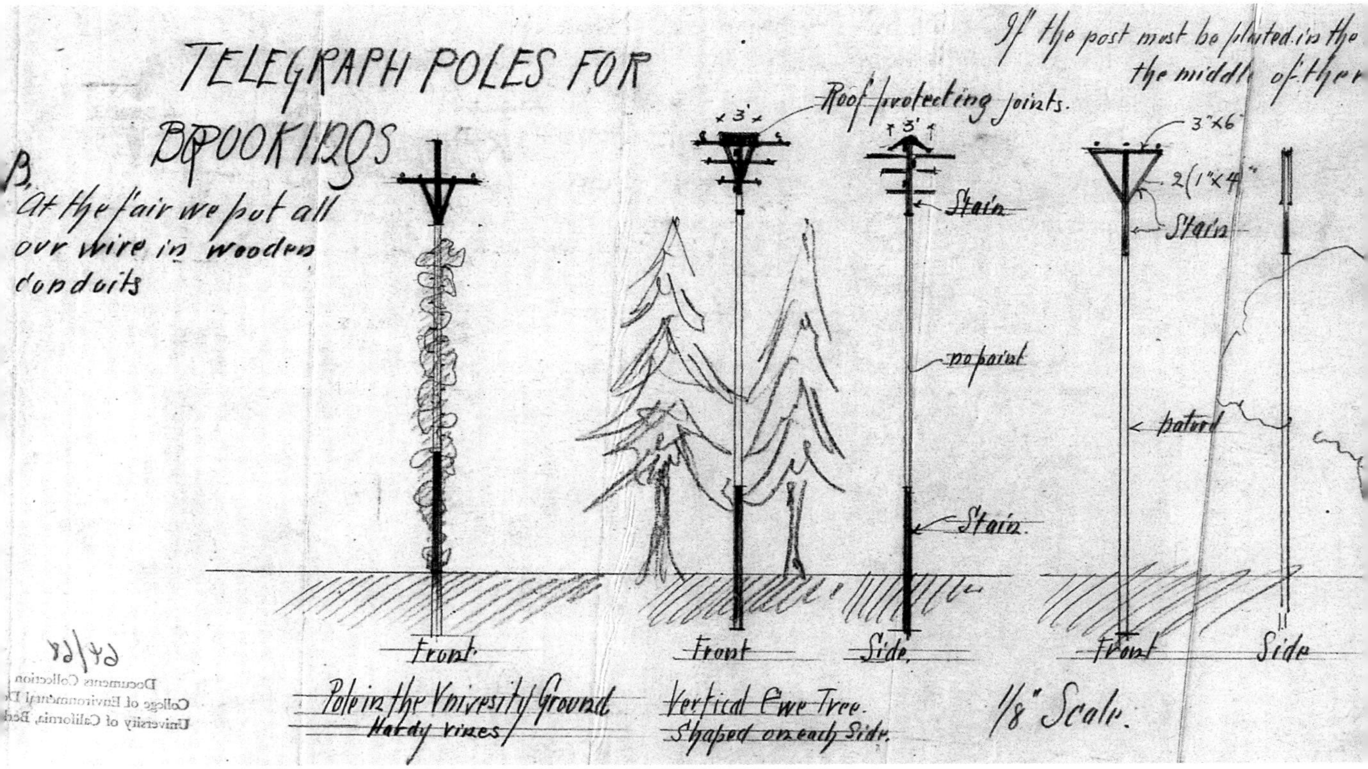

FIGURE 24

TELEGRAPH POLES FOR BROOKINGS, OREGON, 1913.
SECTIONS / ELEVATIONS.
[EDA, UCB]

Among the Reverend Worcester's closest friends and most devoted followers was the successful and prominent Bay Area painter William Keith, whose paintings of the seasons of the Californian landscape still adorn the walls of the Swedenborgian church. Even had Keith not been a close friend of Worcester, Maybeck would eventually have met him and become acquainted with his work, as both were members of the Bohemian Club where Keith regularly exhibited his paintings.[71] Keith and Maybeck had a common vision of the landscape—one that Keith recorded on canvas and that Maybeck created in three dimensions through his architecture and landscapes.

Keith, like Worcester, was a close companion of the Sierra Club founder, John Muir, who took the painter on an early tour of Yosemite, allowing him to become one of the first artists to portray that wilderness [figure 26]. From his friendship with Worcester, Keith gained spiritual guidance. From Muir he gained an expanded

FIGURE 26

GROUP PORTRAIT, 1909.

FROM THE LEFT, STANDING: CHARLES KEELER, WILLIAM KEITH, AND FRANCIS BROWN; *SEATED*: JOHN MUIR AND JOHN BURROUGHS. [THE BANCROFT LIBRARY, UNIVERSITY OF CALIFORNIA, BERKELEY]

FIGURE 28

OAKLAND PACKARD SHOWROOM, OAKLAND, 1928.

[*CALIFORNIA ARTS AND ARCHITECTURE*,
FEBRUARY 1929]

glowed with warmth or a warm color.[77] Jones, and apparently Maybeck, believed the architect could achieve this "bloom" or chromatic harmony so that the building would appear to glow — an effect Maybeck achieved especially well at the Palace of Fine Arts.

Moreover, strong similarities characterize Maybeck's rendering techniques and Keith's landscape paintings, particularly apparent in their delineation of oaks, a favorite subject for both men [figure 29]. This pictorial comparison may at first seem superficial, but it establishes the influence exerted on the architect by prominent local painters like Keith. Maybeck incorporated Keith's techniques and subject matter into his architectural studies and renderings and then attempted to realize those idealized landscapes in three dimensions. The result was a facet of the regional landscape style one might term the "California Picturesque." Although "picturesque" is a complex term with multiple dimensions and associations, here it indicates landscape design that emulates the views portrayed by particular landscape painters.[78]

In Maybeck's often literal pictorial approach, his renderings might feature a garden seen through an architectural aperture. In the Senger house of 1907, for example, the architect permanently attached a painted view of several redwoods to the wall of a dining room alcove by making the frame a part of the wall. The painting faces a glass door that bracketed a nearly identical view of a cluster of redwoods in the garden [figures 30, 31]. Maybeck's early design description specifically mentioned these redwoods as an important garden element.[79] The painting acts as a mirror presenting, again, an idealized version of the garden beyond. Of course, Maybeck's pictorial approach is hardly unprecedented and can be traced back several centuries. But the immediate pictorial base for his work was inspired by the romantic, idealized, Mediterranean ideal of California depicted by landscape painters like William Keith.

FIGURE 29

UNTITLED, 1915. WATERCOLOR RENDERING.
[BERKELEY ART MUSEUM,
UNIVERSITY OF CALIFORNIA, BERKELEY;
GIFT OF MABEL H.DILLINGER]

FIGURE 30

SENGER RESIDENCE, BERKELEY, 1907. M. STRAUSS. PAINTING OF REDWOODS.

[DIANNE HARRIS]

FIGURE 31

SENGER RESIDENCE, BERKELEY, 1907.

VIEW THROUGH THE GLASS DOOR, OPPOSITE THE PAINTING IN THE DINING NOOK, WHICH MAYBECK CALLED AN "ERKER."

[DIANNE HARRIS]

Two additional Bay Area painters may also have contributed to Maybeck's landscape approach. Arthur and Lucia Mathews, whose studio was in the same building as William Keith's in 1906, touched at least the outer edge of Maybeck's circle. In addition to their acquaintance with Keith, the Mathews were friends with John McLaren, then landscape architect for Golden Gate Park, and Maybeck's landscape consultant for the Palace of Fine Arts and for several residences. Lucia Mathews was an avid gardener, and landscape and botanical themes provided the predominant subject matter for both her paintings and decorative arts.[80]

Besides their painting activities, the Mathews owned and operated a shop where they sold furniture of their own design. Their brown-shingled store stylistically resembled Maybeck's residential architecture, suggesting a certain amount of creative exchange.[81] If Maybeck's shingled structures influenced the Mathews, certainly their paintings of the Californian landscape filled with live oaks, pines, cypresses, and fruits, affected the architect as much as did those of William Keith. Maybeck's renderings and the Mathews' paintings show similarities in method of depiction: the same twisted oaks, the same soft-focus Mediterranean romanticism, and a chromatic range that favored warm tones [figure 32]. Maybeck emulated these artists' idealized Californian landscape of vines, flowers, fruit, and woods, first on paper in his preliminary sketches and presentation renderings using pastels, pencils, and ink and later on the project site using earth, plant materials, water, and architecture.

Another important component of Maybeck's visual repertoire was the Yosemite Valley home of the naturalist John Muir. No photographs of Muir's Yosemite dwelling have come to light, but documents describe a structure constructed entirely of wood, with a stream running through the house, and ferns growing through its floor.[82] The house sat adjacent to the Hutchings Hotel of the 1860s where Muir had once been a guest, the lodging famed for the enormous cedar tree that punctured the hotel's living room floor and extended through the roof [figure 33].

FIGURE 32 (*above*)

***YOUTH*, CIRCA 1917. ARTHUR F. MATHEWS.**
[OAKLAND MUSEUM OF CALIFORNIA;
GIFT OF CONCOURS D'ANTIQUES,
THE ART GUILD]

FIGURE 33 (*below*)

**THE BIG TREE ROOM, HUTCHINGS HOTEL,
YOSEMITE VALLEY, CIRCA 1884.**
[THE BANCROFT LIBRARY,
UNIVERSITY OF CALIFORNIA, BERKELEY]

Those early images—approximating a Californian version of the primitive hut given so much attention as the foundations of architectural theory at the École—appear in a number of Maybeck's projects. Although a later example, a pastel drawing on brown paper depicting a forest hut designed for the Golden Gate International Exposition (1936–39) displays a particular charm. A forest scene depicts what Maybeck called a "forest tent of bark," a small, open shelter that could be closed, as his directions below the title instructed the viewer, by simply dropping the suspended roof panel, which was also made of bark [figures 34, 34A].[83]

A deeper examination of a specific project illustrates the importance of this early rustic example. Although bark-covered structures and building parts recur in Maybeck's work, only one such project was fully realized: the Lumbermen's Association building, or House of Hoo-Hoo, designed for San Francisco's Panama Pacific International Exposition of 1915. The building has received far less attention than Maybeck's Palace of Fine Arts though both were important components of the exposition. But if the latter has been called an "immense garden structure," then the House of Hoo-Hoo was literally a building disguised as a landscape.[84] Maybeck designed the lodge for the Lumbermen's Association as an advertisement for their trade and it became one of the not-to-be-missed attractions of the fair. The columns of the building's peristyle and pergola consisted of various logs representing the range of species commercially available on the West Coast. Each log/column ranged in diameter from 24 to 40 inches. Disguised to look like a clump of redwood trees, the House of Hoo-Hoo remains only in a few photographs [figure 35].

Situated in the South Gardens' Forestry Court and facing the Horticultural Palace near the main entrance to the fair, the structure must have created a striking impression. Most prominent were the artificial redwood tree trunks that marked the corners of the building. Requiring 32,000 square feet of 6-inch-thick bark to cover the enormous pylons, each column measured 16 feet in diameter and stood

FIGURE 34

FOREST TENT OF BARK, REDWOOD EMPIRE BUILDING, GOLDEN GATE INTERNATIONAL EXPOSITION, SAN FRANCISCO, 1938. SKETCH.

[EDA, UCB]

FIGURE 34A

FOREST TENT OF BARK, REDWOOD EMPIRE BUILDING, GOLDEN GATE INTERNATIONAL EXPOSITION, SAN FRANCISCO, 1938. SKETCH (DETAIL).

[EDA, UCB]

40 feet high.[85] Section drawings of these stump/pylons show that they were actually constructed from wood studs covered by an outer layer of natural redwood bark. The base of each pylon was to be "covered to look like a root," as specified in the construction drawings, and the structure of each was designed to carry roof-level planter boxes like those Maybeck designed atop the colonnade at the Palace of Fine Arts [figure 36]. These rustic boxes on the lumbermen's lodge created Maybeck's own architectural "order" with vegetative column capitals that literally recalled the stylized acanthus leaves of the Corinthian order.

In a letter to the building committee, the architect requested "30 cypress 8 feet high, 60 trees from 6–8 feet high, and 12 trees 9 feet and over to be planted on top of the pylons and in front of and at the corners of the building." The committee rejected the idea, but Maybeck was successful in obtaining 5,000 vines, trees, and shrubs for use on the site, arguing in a letter to the chair of the building committee that "as you know the planting is the most essential part of the design."[86] Many of these plants were used essentially as camouflage. For example, small redwoods surrounded the bases of the pylon/stumps resembling the secondary growth or suckers that typically emanate from the base of redwoods. As specified on the ground plan, flowers and shrubs formed a screen such that they "covered the redwood bark on the house and imitation trees so a close view cannot be obtained of the fake" [figure 37].

The various elevated planter boxes contained *Lonicera*, *Jasminum primulinum*, *Coronilla glauca*, *Acacia verticillata* and *longifolia*, and *Acacia latifolia*. The side entrances were planted again with the *Acacia verticillata* and with *Fuchsia gracilis*. Behind the structure, Maybeck dedicated separate planting beds to the display of ferns and perennials, combining *Athyrium filix-femina* with *Aspidium aculeatum*, *Heuchera micrantha*, *rubescens*, and *sanguinea*, *Astilbe japonica*, *Boykinia*, *Lilium humboldtii*, *Anemone japonica*, *Epimedium*, *Tellima grandiflora*, *Thalictrum delavayi*, and *Cymbalaria muralis*. For a vivid floral display that would have

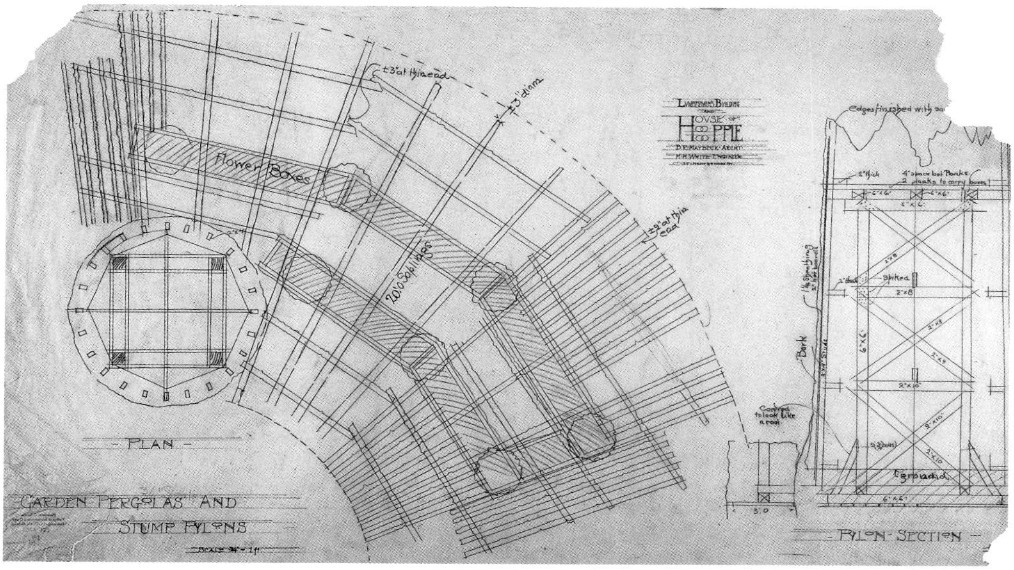

FIGURE 35 *(above)*

THE LUMBERMEN'S BUILDING, OR HOUSE OF HOO-HOO, PANAMA PACIFIC INTERNATIONAL EXPOSITION, SAN FRANCISCO, 1915.

[*WESTERN ARCHITECT*, SEPTEMBER 1915]

FIGURE 36 *(below)*

LUMBERMEN'S BUILDING, OR HOUSE OF HOO-HOO, 1915. DRAWING OF GARDEN PERGOLAS AND STUMP PYLONS; PLAN AND SECTION.

[EDA, UCB]

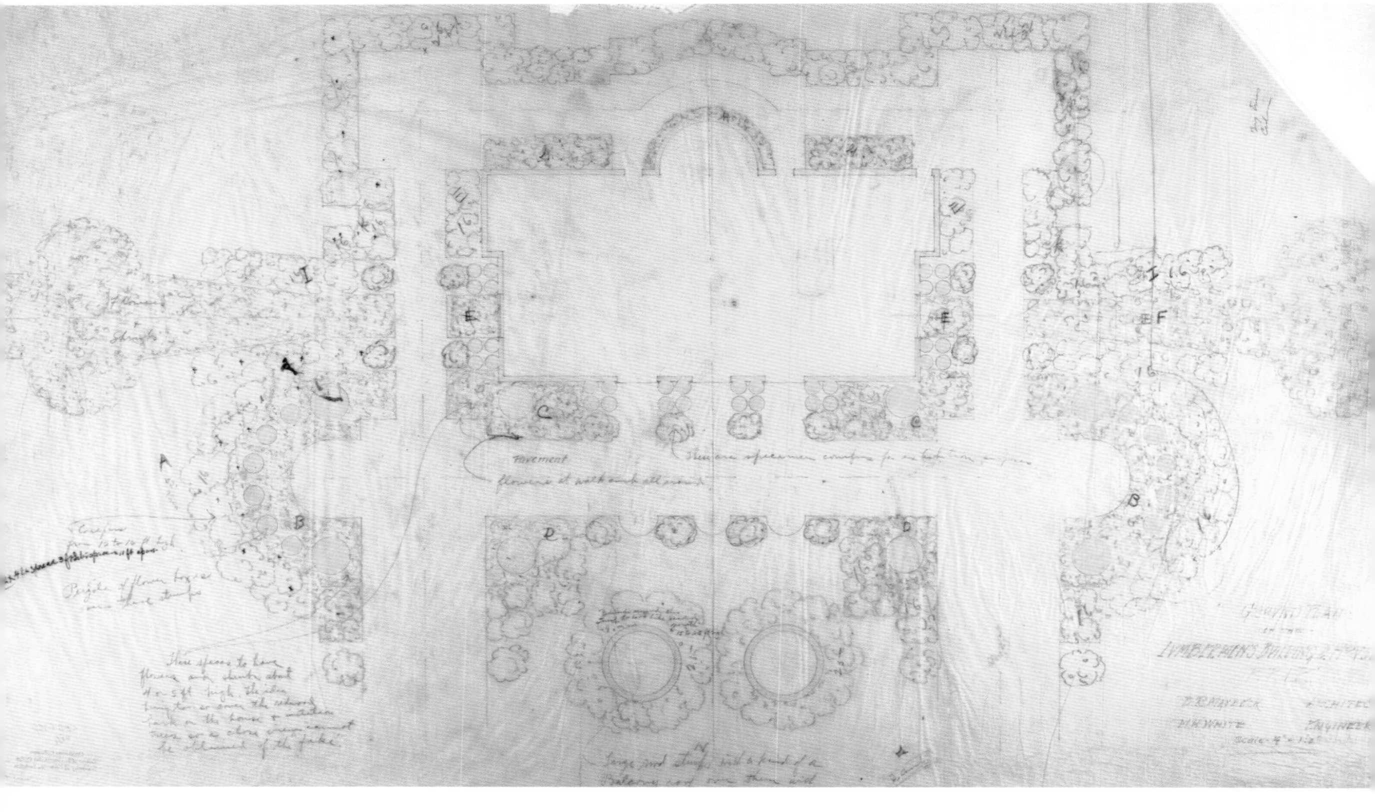

FIGURE 37

LUMBERMEN'S BUILDING, OR HOUSE OF HOO-HOO, 1915. GROUND PLAN WITH PLANTING.

[EDA, UCB]

recalled more naturalistically the bedded-out plantings found elsewhere at the fair, he added varieties of sunflower, coreopsis, helianthus, wallflowers, goldenrod, and gaillardia to the mix above.[87]

Completed in 1914 for a total cost of $20,000, the unusual building had great charm and appeal. In 1915 Ben Macomber described it as "a sylvan idyll, telling of lofty trees, cool shades, and secret bowers of fern and vine and wild flower, in the moist and tangled redwood forests. There is little used but rough-barked tree trunks, but what delicate harmony and arrangement!"[88] Maybeck's scenographic manipulations were clever enough to fool Macomber into believing the stumps to be authentic whole trunks, and despite its eccentricity, the arrangement was sufficiently artful to garner the praise of the numerous critics who viewed the pavilion. The House of Hoo-Hoo was both whimsical and romantic—Maybeck's version of a primitive hut that likewise evoked Muir's rough-hewn wood cabin. The design evoked the "charm, poetry and sentiment of the forest," ideas deeply ingrained in Maybeck's turn-of-the-century landscape sensibility.[89]

Clearly, Maybeck was enmeshed in contemporary attitudes toward architecture and landscape design, both locally and internationally. The sheer volume of quickly sketched studies that accompany nearly all his design development drawings attest to his unswerving interest in the development of spaces beyond the building's walls. Vegetation is everywhere in these studies, drawn rapidly on tracing paper or brown paper with chalk pastels or colored pencil, at times overwhelming the very buildings the architect was seeking to promote. His interest was persistent; an impulse for landscape design that resulted in some clever and unique solutions to the question of the common ground that exists between indoors and out.

LANDSCAPE AS BOTH FIGURE AND GROUND

> *Bernard Maybeck, the Berkeley architect, had long been telling California that architecture here, to be beautiful, needed only to be an effective background for landscape. His theory is that as trees and plants grow so easily and so quickly here, Californians are wasting their finest source of beauty if they do not combine landscape with building.*
>
> Ben Macomber, 1915

A set of identifiable and characteristic approaches for integrating specific landscape elements or materials with their architectural setting and for integrating a building with its site underlies all Maybeck's landscape work. The importance of Maybeck's outdoor work lies less in the landscape designed as a separate entity with an identifiable style of its own than in the relation of the landscape to his architecture. He did not normally strive to create gardens or landscapes as separate entities. Rather, the form and style of the garden are site- and architecture-specific, determined by the individual nature of each project. A look at specific projects brings those structural strategies into sharper focus.

Maybeck held fast to the tradition—derived from his education at the École—of creating elegant compositions, and his plans sometimes resembled designs for pieces of jewelry.[90] But instead of the traditional conception of architecture as figure and landscape as ground, Maybeck frequently treated both as equally figural. Only empty space became "ground." In so doing, he subverted the frequently held assumption that landscape is transparent or even invisible. Because landscape mattered so much to him, and because he normally conceived architecture and garden as a single and unified compositional whole, vegetation frequently became at least symbolically "concrete" for Maybeck. A number of his projects demonstrate the point. His "Aeroplane perspective" drawing for his 1931 general plan of the Principia College campus includes an informal grouping of buildings on the site along with plantings

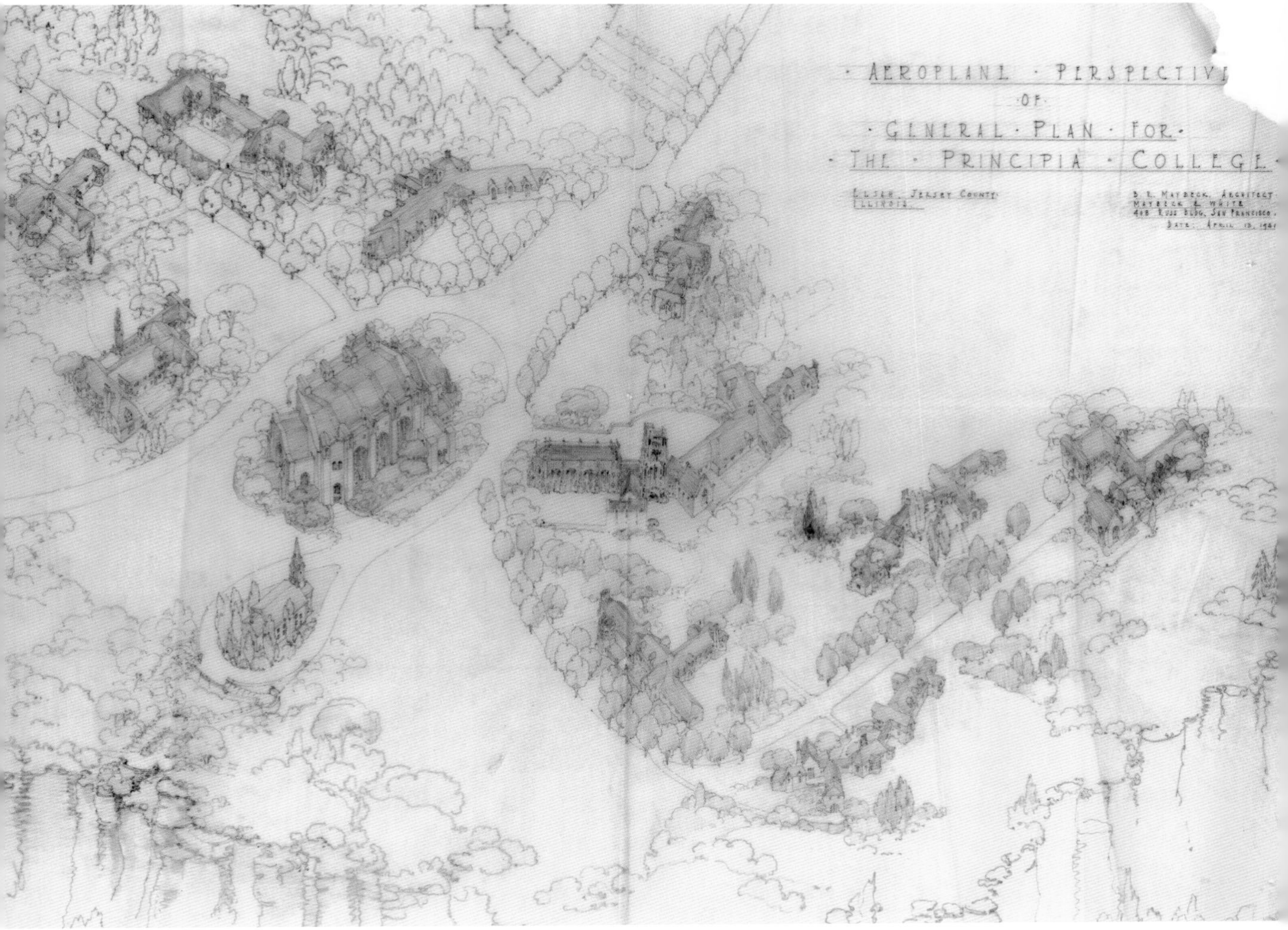

FIGURE 38

PRINCIPIA COLLEGE, ELSAH, ILLINOIS, 1931.
"AEROPLANE PERSPECTIVE."
[EDA, UCB]

and road alignments. But more detailed drawings include the architect's darkly drawn contour lines that helped him site building groups appropriately to the shape of the land.[91] These practices, one could argue, are simply those of the conscientious designer. Yet everything on Maybeck's site plans appears to receive equal weight as a subject for study [figure 38]. The even-handed quality of the drawings can make it difficult to discern a hierarchy of parts since the buildings are not compositionally privileged as they would normally appear in such renderings. In fact, in some early studies for the campus, the landscape receives greater embellishment and elaboration than the architecture.

A statement written by Maybeck to clarify his design approach for the Palace of Fine Arts makes explicit his use of landscape as compositional figure rather than as ground. He wrote,

> *Usually in good planning, when the plan of the walls of the building are blacked in on paper the picture thus made is agreeable to the eye. To get this result in the Fine Arts Plan, the shrubs were used to fill the vacancies that usually are filled out with walls, which are called "points de pocher." I do not mention the above in the light of an apology, but rather wish to show that those who plan in snow countries have a different problem from our California architects.*[92]

By acknowledging again the special qualities of the region in which he worked and the importance of its temperate climate, Maybeck strengthened the Mediterranean imagery, as well as affirming the notion of green architecture in his conception of the use of vegetation as *pocher* [figure 39].

Almost none of this green architecture remains at the Palace of Fine Arts today [figure 40]. Originally, blooming plants, shrubs, and small acacia trees appeared between the columns of the peristyle. In their place a few acanthus grow, recalling the stylized Corinthian capitals above. Purple-leaf plums create a striking contrast to the ocher concrete, providing a flickering visual effect that enhances the structure's presence.

At Maybeck's First Church of Christ, Scientist, in Berkeley, the most prominent landscape feature is an enormous coast redwood, which now towers over the church at the corner of the site [figure 41]. The redwood anchors the site, but Jacomena Maybeck, the architect's daughter-in-law, implied in her published memoir that the tree was planted to serve as a steeple for the church, which otherwise has none.[93] Although Maybeck did not include traditional steeples in his designs for the Unitarian Church in Palo Alto (1906, no longer extant) or for the Ninth Church of Christ, Scientist in San Francisco (unbuilt), Jacomena Maybeck's speculation seems plausible in view of the architect's interest in the design of the steeple for his Principia College chapel many years later [figure 42]. The redwood tree-as-steeple serves as another example of landscape used as figure instead of ground. The tree forms a strong, assertive, and monumental figural mass that is central to the church's exterior composition.

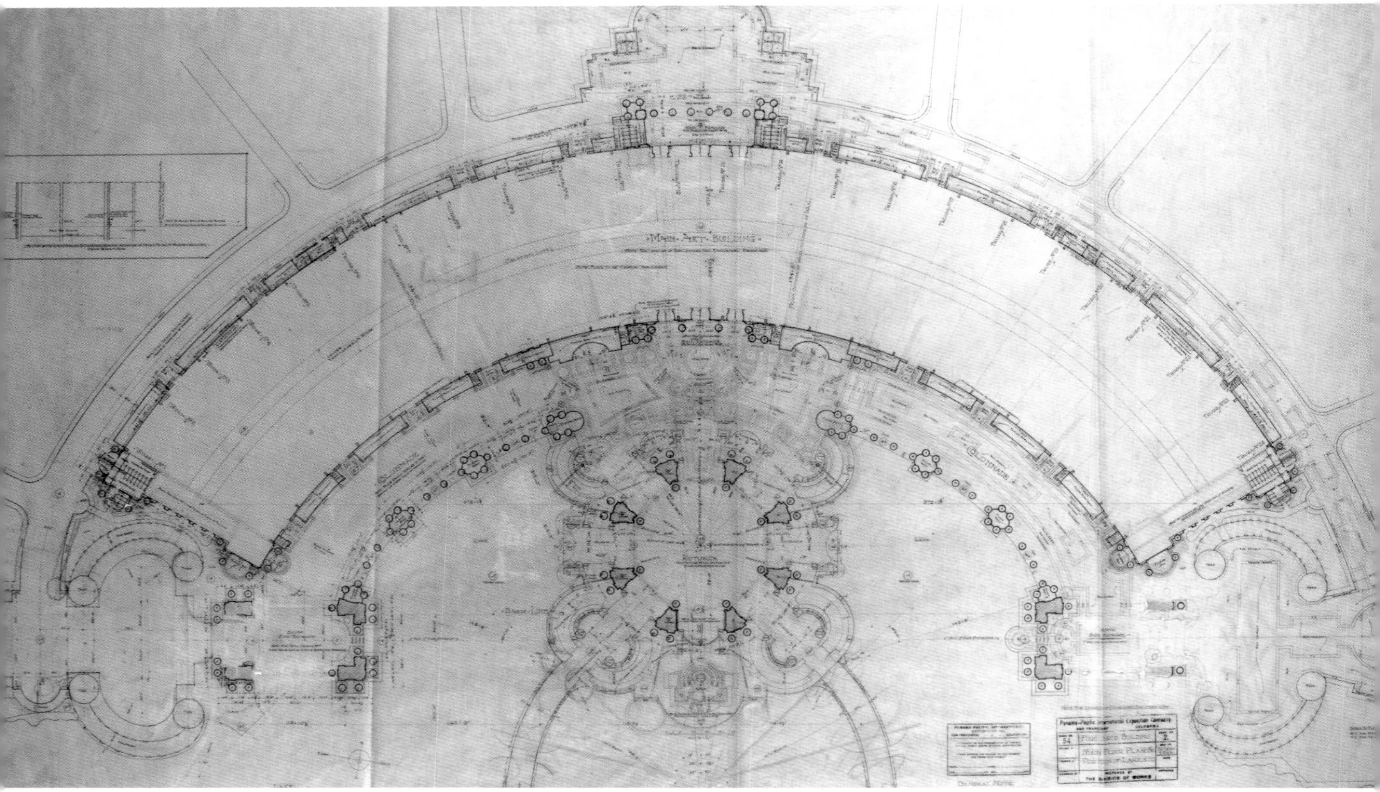

FIGURE 39

PALACE OF FINE ARTS, SAN FRANCISCO, 1915.
GROUND PLAN WITH PLANTING.
[EDA, UCB]

FIGURE 40

PALACE OF FINE ARTS, SAN FRANCISCO.
RECENT VIEW.
[MARC TREIB]

FIGURE 41

THE REDWOOD STEEPLE, FIRST CHURCH OF CHRIST, SCIENTIST, BERKELEY.

[DIANNE HARRIS]

FIGURE 42 (*opposite*)

CHAPEL, PRINCIPIA COLLEGE, CIRCA 1926. RENDERING.

[GEORGE COOKE, THE PRINCIPIA]

may seem for an institutional building—a hospital no less—it generated a concept for the design of a humane medical complex taking advantage of the conditions of the site and surrounding landscape.

A bird's-eye view of the hospital included a series of linear pavilions arranged to create landscaped courtyards [figure 44]. An arch marked the entry to the complex accompanied by a column "topped by a winged figure that looked toward Mt. Sutro and across the buildings placed unobtrusively against the hillside."[96] The wards extended into the northern slope of Mt. Sutro; the planting in the drawing mitigated the effect of the large building complex on the site. The courtyard arrangement would have maximized ventilation, as the design and orientation of the wards maximized sunlight. Lighting was of particular importance to Maybeck for this scheme because he believed that northern light, enhanced by its reflection on the nearby ocean, would make an excellent source of natural illumination for the surgical amphitheater, which was to have glass walls.

Whether or not the ideas were practical, these features again suggest Maybeck's awareness of the qualities of the region and his ability to use the attributes of the landscape to enhance his architecture. Part of the appeal of the hospital scheme stems from its Italianate style that recalls to a greater degree Mediterranean villas than antiseptic tiled hallways and clinics. The tiled roofs, the clusters of oaks, the landscape dotted with lawns and punctuated by Italian cypress, reveal Maybeck's consuming Mediterranean sensibility, which he applied consistently to any building type. The pavilion and courtyard design also revealed the architect's belief in the healing, healthful aspects of nature and the garden. If indoor-outdoor living promoted health, certainly it would make sense to design a hospital that had a strong connection to the outdoors as well.[97]

The 1925 design for the Hearst Memorial Gymnasium on the University of California, Berkeley campus, manifests a similar desire to merge landscape into a large building mass through the creation of multiple courtyards. The level of Maybeck's involvement on this project remains somewhat uncertain since it was a collaborative effort between Maybeck and Julia Morgan, with John Gregg acting as landscape consultant. Morgan's office prepared the construction documents, but Maybeck's design influence remains clear in many of the building's components and details. Like Maybeck, Morgan frequently implemented courtyard schemes; those found at the gymnasium recall her enclosed patios in the Berkeley City Club as well as those in Oakland's Chapel of the Chimes. In each case, the courtyards admit diffuse light and fresh air to the lower level and interior spaces of the building, with small gardens punctuating the architectural mass. At the gym, the courtyards relieve the otherwise institutional quality of long corridors and locker rooms, a constant reminder to users of their connection to the outdoors and of the healthful benefits of exercise in the fresh air. Although the plan derives from Beaux-Arts models known to both architects, it remains distinctly Californian and shows Maybeck's influence, particularly in its planting.[98]

The dominant plant used at the gymnasium is the California live oak, more characteristic of the University of California campus for Maybeck and his contemporaries such as William Keith, than the pollarded plane trees we now associate with the campus landscape. Maybeck used these oaks pervasively at the gymnasium; a small grove appears in one of the courtyards, groupings grow on the raised terraces at the second-story level, and again in the planter boxes (decorated with toga-clad women) on the pool terrace. The oaks near the pool no longer exist; they died and were not replaced because their leaves littered the terrace and fell into the white marble swimming pool. But they were an important part of the design for the architect, who sketched the trees repeatedly and corresponded with Gregg to gather information on the soil conditions necessary for the survival of oaks growing in contained areas on a terrace [figures 45, 46].[99] The drawing includes his typical color scheme: orange, Tuscan red, yellow, and pink. Moreover, it indicates the importance of the reflection of both building and landscape in a body of water, in this case the extraordinary swimming pool.

The fact that Maybeck controlled the gymnasium landscape design is evident in another letter from Gregg to Maybeck. Regarding Maybeck's planting plan for the area west of the pool, which was to have been enclosed by a balustrade, Gregg wrote, "If this plan meets with your approval, I will be very glad to proceed with a more detailed study. If I have failed to interpret your ideas, I would be very glad to consult with you further concerning the treatment of this area."[100] The designing pencil was clearly Maybeck's—in short, he conceived the landscape and architecture together, as one composition.

The courtyard appears again, at a residential scale, in Maybeck's 1920 design for the James J. Fagan residence in Woodside, California. Also labeled "Woodside Oaks" on some drawings, Maybeck's design divided the house into two separate wings, one containing bedrooms and private spaces, the other, living and shared spaces. An elliptical court between them became the central space of the residence [figures 47, 48]. The plan literally forced the Fagan family to move between indoor and outdoor spaces as they conducted everyday activities—in rainy weather or in sunshine—blurring the distinction between architecture and landscape. Indeed, the court's position suggests that the family substituted outdoor for indoor living whenever possible, establishing a significant precedent for the ideal Californian lifestyle promoted countless times in later decades. This plan arrangement clearly appealed to the architect; it appears again in one of his undated sketches for Hillside Houses in Berkeley (circa 1900)—a courtyard covered with a trellis literally bisects the simple dwelling [figure 49].[101]

FIGURE 45 *(above)*

HEARST MEMORIAL GYMNASIUM, 1926.
BERNARD MAYBECK WITH JULIA MORGAN.
THE RENDERING INDICATES THE PLANTING INTENDED FOR THE POOL AREA.
[EDA, UCB]

FIGURE 45 *(above)*

HEARST GYMNASIUM SWIMMING POOL, WITH PLANTING.
[THE BANCROFT LIBRARY, UNIVERSITY OF CALIFORNIA, BERKELEY]

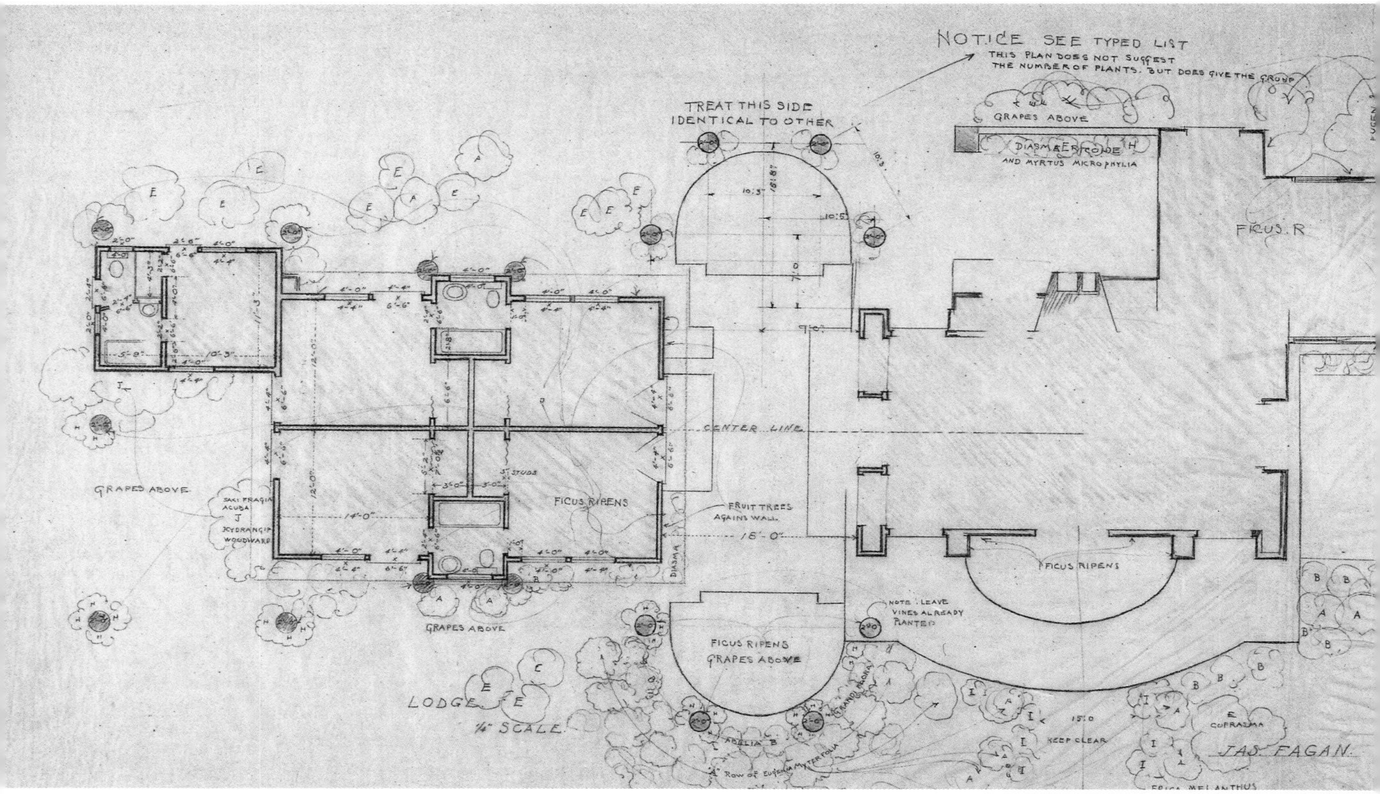

FIGURE 47

JAMES J. FAGAN RESIDENCE, WOODSIDE, 1920.
GROUND PLAN WITH PLANTING.

[EDA, UCB]

FIGURE 48

JAMES J. FAGAN RESIDENCE, CIRCA 1928. VIEW OF COURTYARD.

[EDA, UCB]

Adjacent to the Fagans' main living room, Maybeck provided two alcoves containing beds that could be rolled into the courtyard, and each sleeping area had its own trellis-covered terrace. Here again, landscape and architecture receive equal weight, the ratio of enclosed and open rooms nearly equivalent in the plan. Paved in subtle shades of pink concrete, the court's Mediterranean allusions are unmistakable, yet it remains distinctly Californian in terms of its relation to the interior spaces and planting. Maybeck grouped the vegetation informally, yet the massing nonetheless reinforces the architectural plan. He specified areas to be kept clear to preserve views from the interior, as well as areas of dense planting to enclose and shelter the court, substituting heavy planting for walls in this outdoor room—another example of planting as *pocher*.

Although John McLaren served as landscape consultant on the Fagan residence, it is clear from the correspondence in the Fagan job file as well as from the architect's drawings, that Maybeck's hand created the landscape scheme for the house and that

FIGURE 49

HILLSIDE HOME, CIRCA 1900. DRAWING.

IN THIS STUDY, THE HOUSE IS DIVIDED BY A CENTRAL COURTYARD.

[EDA, UCB]

he made the first recommendations for plant selection. He then asked McLaren for recommendations on the number and species of plants that would be necessary to achieve his desired effects.

The general site plan indicated a large lawn enclosed by an irregular border of tea trees, acacia, oleander, viburnum, *Hypericum calycinum*, and cotoneaster. An orchard composed of thirty-two trees (species unspecified) abutted a large vegetable garden near the barn.[102] The plants selected to effect the courtyard enclosure were thoughtfully chosen, though whether by McLaren or Maybeck remains unclear; Maybeck's handwriting appears on the drawing for the house and courtyard plan. To surround and enclose the court he chose *Abelia grandiflora* and *Eugenia myrtifolia* (*Syzygium paniculatum*), both effective visual barriers that flower or fruit in winter in shades of purple or pink, reinforcing the color scheme of his paving [figure 50]. In this garden, Maybeck showed a preference for winter-blooming plants and for drought-tolerant species in his selection of coprosma, heath, myrtle, and aucuba.

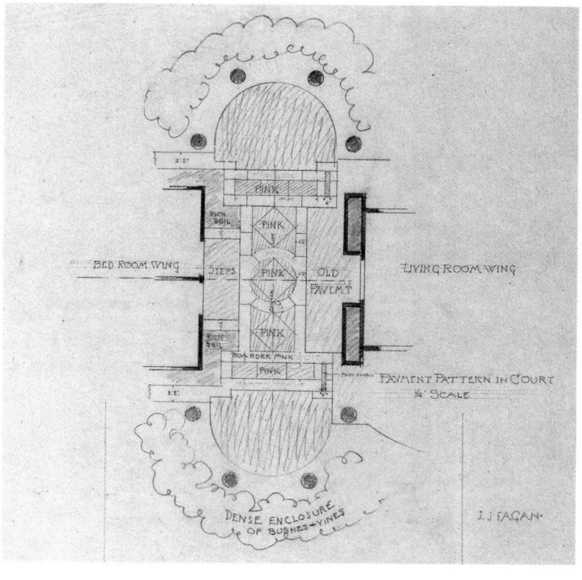

FIGURE 50

JAMES J. FAGAN RESIDENCE, WOODSIDE, 1920.
PLAN OF COURT.
[EDA, UCB]

Characteristic of his work, Maybeck's use of these plants demonstrates an interest in achieving a year-round cycle of bloom. He placed the shade-tolerant aucuba on the northern side of the house, while specifying fruit trees to grow against the sheltered southern wall of the courtyard. Atop the numerous trellises that extend from the house, Maybeck specified grapes rather than his trademark wisteria, but to similar effect. Both vines are appropriate material for the region: they create shade during the warm summer months and defoliate in winter, allowing the sun to penetrate and warm both indoor and outdoor spaces. The grape vines also neatly emphasize the design's Mediterranean allusions.

The Fagan residence, with its courtyard plan, became one of several important models for indoor-outdoor living in California of the 1920s—truly "landscape gardening around a few rooms for use in case of rain."[103] [figure 51]. It also provided one of the most complete examples of Maybeck's residential garden designs, showing the architect to have been entirely at ease when faced with the task of plant selection and application.

FIGURE 51

JAMES J. FAGAN RESIDENCE, WOODSIDE, 1920.

VIEW OF TRELLIS.

[EDA, UCB]

DRAWING IN NATURE

The play on words here is intentional: Maybeck literally drew the landscape into his buildings using a variety of visual and constructed techniques, but he also drew it into his renderings on the page. Many architects add entourage to a drawing when it is nearly finished, using vegetation to soften the building's lines, to provide a sense of scale, and to add visual appeal. Maybeck's work differs from this model, with landscape appearing ubiquitously, in sketches and drawings made at all stages of the design process.

In many respects, drawing in amounted to an act of framing. For example, many of Maybeck's interior renderings include detailed elaboration of the plants that were to be viewed through the windows. Hence the landscape became a picture, captured and framed by the architecture. In a section drawing through the assembly hall for the unbuilt Ninth Church of Christ, Scientist (1935–37), Maybeck rendered raised blinds on the windows to reveal the planting he painted to appear outside the windows. He clearly considered the planting as a part of the building's ornament, a framed and dynamic picture for the interior [see figure 66]. Likewise, numerous studies for both the Phoebe Apperson Hearst Memorial and the Palace of Fine Arts included brightly rendered landscape bracketed by architectural components. Because he rendered the landscape in brilliant pastel tones, in these drawings the muted architecture appears as a modest, albeit elegant, border that focuses our vision on the forms and spaces that lie beyond [figure 52]. Again, the drawing's compositional hierarchy resists conventional modes of representation: the architecture is more elaborately detailed and rendered with exacting line-work, but the landscape is far more vivid and rich, competing effectively for the viewer's attention. The eye moves back and forth, from the frame to the framed and back again, in an oscillating pattern that neatly reflects the equal attention paid these subjects by the architect.

FIGURE 52

PHOEBE APPERSON HEARST MEMORIAL, UNIVERSITY OF CALIFORNIA, BERKELEY, 1928. RENDERING.

[EDA, UCB]

By placing either a sculpturally significant shrub or tree or a dramatically colorful planting before the main window(s) of his buildings, Maybeck again took a pictorial approach that visually drew the landscape into his buildings. Here, vegetation served essentially as either sculpture or impressionistic color. For example, at the Kennedy house and studio in Berkeley (1923), a twisted, dramatic *Leptospermum* acts as a sculptural subject outside the main window of the recital hall, which is also the prominent window on the street facade. At Principia College, the bright pink color of eastern redbuds appears outside the main windows of some campus buildings during their dramatic, spring bloom.

At the Leon Roos residence, a mixed border of vivid annuals and perennials creates an impressionistic wash of color in front of the leaded dining room window along the street frontage. By rendering his scheme in watercolor on a blueprint, Maybeck removed any ambiguity about his intent for this garden [figure 53]. The garden consisted of a flower border, some shrubs, and a small area of lawn, all enclosed by a clipped hedge. By increasing the density of the planting and using taller vegetation in front of the leaded windows, he thereby created his own "stained glass," using the planting outside diagonally leaded panes to achieve an impressionistic, subtle effect of color and light. The diagonal pattern of leading matches the diagonal pattern of the lattice implemented on the adjacent gate, once again cleverly connecting house and garden.

Although the vast majority of Maybeck's work is spatially rich, this particular approach represents a flattened, two-dimensional landscape sensibility, perhaps reflecting the architect's attempt to simulate as nearly as possible the landscapes framed by Keith and the Mathews in their paintings. Still, this approach manipulates a series of two-dimensional planes to create a three-dimensional effect, using layers composed of frame, window, and vegetation to build a composite scene.

FIGURE 53

LEON ROOS RESIDENCE, SAN FRANCISCO, 1909.

THIS WATERCOLORED PRINT OF THE ELEVATION
INDICATES MAYBECK'S INTENTIONS
FOR THE FRONT GARDEN.
[EDA, UCB]

GREEN WALLS AND FOUNDATIONS

In Maybeck's designs, clipped evergreen hedges frequently define a garden's edge, with low, green walls framing the buildings. Whether an edge or a base, this gives the effect of a green foundation, tying or "rooting" the structure to the landscape. At the Town and Gown Club in Berkeley (1899), boxwood traces the limits of the site; at the Roos house it follows the foundation line of the house, stepping down the hill [figure 54]. At the First Church of Christ, Scientist, in Berkeley, *Ficus repens* (creeping fig) covers the low concrete walls that form both the surrounding planter beds and the foundation for the church. As William Jordy has pointed out, this verdant base serves to anchor the building to the soil and at the same time acts to "mitigate the squeeze of the building on its limited site."[104] The vine visually obscures the building's edge, effacing the line between the church's architectural boundaries and the landscape, thereby visually expanding the space.

Most dramatic, perhaps, were the green walls that seemed to rise out of the lagoon at the Palace of Fine Arts [figure 55]. Though eliminated when the Palace was reconstructed in permanent materials, these vertical surfaces of vegetation, which Ben Macomber described as "semi-circular walls of growing *Mesembryanthemum*" (ice plant), contributed to the visual effect of a palace that seemed literally to grow directly from the water. Although the 1915 exhibition officially celebrated the opening of the Panama canal, it equally (though somewhat less explicitly) celebrated San Francisco's phoenixlike emergence from the ashes of the devastating 1906 earthquake and fire.[105] The fair's grounds and buildings served as a built example of the city's remarkable recovery. In his 1916 retrospective tribute to the exhibition, Louis J. Stellmann wrote of "the trees that arose from bogs, French gardens from wastes and mires, fountains and pools from ditches and sloughs."[106] In fact Maybeck designed the Palace of Fine Arts to appear as though it too were emerging magically from the surrounding waters, and the green terraces provided a verdant base that enhanced this desired appearance. This element also helped connect the Palace of Fine Arts to one of the most significant landscape features at the fair: John McLaren's massive green wall that bordered the entire length of the South Gardens. Described as being "three times the height of a man," the wall was composed of thousands of small planter boxes set closely together and planted with more *Mesembryanthemum* to create a solid mass of vertical vegetation. Since one of the chief design objectives for the fair was to integrate landscape and architecture as a balanced composition throughout, Maybeck and McLaren likely used these green verticals as one element in an attempt to tie together a larger planning effort.[107]

FIGURE 54

LEON ROOS RESIDENCE, SAN FRANCISCO.

[MARC TREIB]

TRELLISES AND PERGOLAS

Among Maybeck's most frequently used devices, trellises and pergolas supporting vines (usually wisteria) appeared often enough in his work to be considered a distinguishing characteristic. Instead of simply attaching them to the outside of the building, Maybeck almost always designed them as an outgrowth of the building's structural system. By extending beams or rafters from the roof system of the house, and cross-layering them with smaller pieces of lumber, the architect achieved his desired effects of shade and shadow. In one instance, the Fagan residence, a trellis substituted for a roof to define other outdoor living spaces over portions of the central courtyard. But this type of structure also appears as an elevated ceiling in his rendering for the Strawberry Canyon bathhouse of 1911 and constructed in his Clyde worker's housing of 1918–19 [figures 56, 57].

In Maybeck's painted rendering for the unbuilt bathhouse, the swimming pool reflects the large vine-covered trellis that hovers as a canopy over the structure, rather than the structure itself. Thus, the trellis becomes the dominant feature of the rendering—the viewer is asked to read it twice. This trellis is unusual for Maybeck because it stands free of the building's structural members and lacks the vines that often hang in front of the windows. He might have intended the hovering vine canopy to serve as a passive solar device because the roof was to slide open on tracks. Or, perhaps the architect simply raised the trellis structure in order to gain the height necessary to achieve the desired reflection in the pool—though he could easily have raised the entire roof to that level and did not. In front of the bathhouse, Maybeck designed a water garden with a fountain and small pool that spilled into the larger swimming pool.[108] As a garden pavilion of glazed facades, views from the interior focused on pool and landscape. A golden tone dominates the rendering, creating an atmosphere of Mediterranean warmth.

FIGURE 55 *(opposite)*

PALACE OF FINE ARTS, SAN FRANCISCO, 1915.
THIS HAND-COLORED IMAGE
DISPLAYS THE GREEN WALLS
THAT SAT AT THE BASE OF THE STRUCTURE.
[*THAT WAS A DREAM WORTH BUILDING*]

Maybeck's trellis structures served four purposes. First, they affected a significant transition between architecture and landscape by extending the building into the garden and by allowing the garden to literally creep up onto the architecture. Second, the structures, with their vines, manifested Maybeck's Mediterranean fantasy by recalling the vineyards of the Italian countryside and the significance of the vine as a symbol of southern fruitfulness. Third, trellises and pergolas contributed to the desired affect of building-as-ruin. Maybeck was enamored with the image of Piranesian ruins covered with plant life that seemed to reclaim the architecture. His trellises can therefore be regarded as fragments of hanging gardens that strengthen the creation of this romantic idea. The long trellises that adorned the rooftop of the exhibition hall at the Palace of Fine Arts were an important element of that composition [figure 58]. Covered with flowers, Maybeck called them a "direct bribe" to appeal to the public, but he also ranked their importance above the palace structure itself, which he called "a mere background for the water, the trees, and the plants on the terraces walls and pergolas."[109] The planted and blooming length of pergolas on the rooftops further contributed to the effect of a structure overgrown by plant life, lending the sense of melancholy the architect hoped to inspire.

Likewise, the broken pediment of a gabled roof, which he implemented at the First Church of Christ, Scientist in Berkeley—as well as at the Wallen Maybeck and Senger residences—produced the impression of structural decay (which Maybeck viewed romantically); the timbers of the pergolas contributed to this effect, appearing almost as compound fractures through the skin of the building.

Finally, the trellises, placed adjacent to or over windows, allowed the vines and blossoms to hang in front of the translucent or transparent glass. With the view through the window as his painting, Maybeck achieved both his desired pictorial scene and affected the light within his architecture. As the sun penetrates the wisteria for example, it casts either a slightly green or purple glow—depending on the time

FIGURE 56

STRAWBERRY CANYON BATHHOUSE, 1911 (UNBUILT).
RENDERING.
[EDA, UCB]

FIGURE 57

WORKER'S HOUSING, CLYDE, 1918–19.

[EDA, UCB]

FIGURE 58

THE PERGOLA MAYBECK DESIGNED AT THE PALACE OF FINE ARTS IS VISIBLE AT THE TOP OF THE STRUCTURE IN THE BACKGROUND.

[*THE JEWEL CITY*]

of year—contributing to the building's overall color scheme. These intentions are made explicit in his drawings for the unbuilt Ninth Church of Christ, Scientist in which the windows are painted the same cast of purple as the wisteria hanging in front of them, as well as by the First Church of Christ, Scientist in Berkeley with its lavender glazing, purple interior lighting scheme, and vigorously growing wisteria [figure 59]. At the latter site, Maybeck's planting plan called for wisteria growing on the main pergola, but it also appears on the church's columns and trellis in an early, colored chalk axonometric drawing, so the vine's inclusion dates from the early phases of design.

FIGURE 59

WISTERIA IN BLOOM, FIRST CHURCH OF CHRIST, SCIENTIST, BERKELEY.

[DIANNE HARRIS]

PLANTER BOXES

Maybeck's frequent inclusion of planter boxes on his buildings was another design feature proposed in Charles Keeler's book and they constitute another of the architect's trademarks. Keeler wrote that "hanging baskets containing vines or ferns are most effective on porches, while boxes of earth may stand on upper balconies from which vines may grow and trail over the outer walls."[110] Attached to the Roos residence, placed on top of columns at the Palace of Fine Arts and House of Hoo-Hoo, and set atop a terrace at the Hearst gymnasium, the planters were characteristically supported on extended horizontal structural members of the building. In an unsuccessful early example, Maybeck attached planter boxes with cypress trees to the side of the Phoebe Apperson Hearst Reception Hall, built in 1899 (but destroyed by fire). The tiny trees appear dwarfed by the monumentality of the structure, contributing nothing to its massing or design [figure 60]. They did indicate, however, an early attempt to soften architectural profiles using vegetation brought literally onto the upper levels of the building.

The Roos house presented a more successful example of this strategy. Here Maybeck linked the house to the garden with flower boxes suspended beneath the windows and along the large front loggia entry. Structural beams extended from the basement under the living room, and the porch beams over the entrance supported the flower boxes. In this way, the structural system of the house ties the garden to it.

For the First Church of Christ, Scientist in Berkeley and the Palace of Fine Arts in San Francisco, enormous planter boxes stood atop groups of columns creating, in effect, a new "order" with actual vegetation serving as a column capital. Had the attic-level boxes atop the colonnade at the Palace of Fine Arts been planted as Maybeck wished, the sculptures of the inward-looking female figures might have appeared somewhat less mysterious [figures 61, 62]. The vines and shrubs that

Maybeck planned to cascade from the boxes would have partially obscured the figures, but at least they might have seemed to gaze into their own microcosmic version of a contained Californian landscape, just as visitors to the exposition reveled in the visual luxury of the larger landscape John McLaren had created for them. Budget cuts prevented realizing Maybeck's planting scheme for the boxes, much to his great disappointment. The lack of those raised plantings, in the architect's view, diminished the accelerated "aged" quality of the design he so desired. Maybeck, however, was quite pleased with the slow decay of his original plaster Palace of Fine Arts, and he hoped, in fact, that redwoods would be planted around the rotunda so that even as it crumbled, the redwoods would grow and eventually overwhelm the structure.[111] Nature would supersede culture and its architecture.

FIGURE 60

PHOEBE APPERSON HEARST RECEPTION HALL, BERKELEY, 1899.

NOTE THE PLANTER BOXES ATTACHED TO THE SIDE AT THE BUILDING'S UPPER LEVEL.

[EDA, UCB]

FIGURE 61

PALACE OF FINE ARTS, SAN FRANCISCO, 1915.
IN THIS DRAWING, THE ARCHITECT HAS SKETCHED IN THE PLANTING HE INTENDED FOR THE ATTIC-LEVEL PLANTER BOXES.
[EDA, UCB]

FIGURE 62

THE PALACE OF FINE ARTS, SAN FRANCISCO.
PLANTER BOXES
[DIANNE HARRIS]

COLOR

Although not always considered as such, manipulation of color is an essential aspect of landscape design. The varied hues of vegetation, natural and electric lighting, painted surfaces, and reflected color from water and other surfaces profoundly shape visual experience in the landscape. The chromatic vibrancy of much Maybeck architecture can be startling. Although the prevalence of wood—shingles, timbers, and paneling —in his residential projects presents a muted and even dark visual effect, the architect seldom overlooked an opportunity to introduce stronger colors. Whether Prussian blue window frames, a splash of color on a detail, pigments integrated into concrete, or in a rich coating of stucco, color was an essential aspect of his work. As mentioned previously, Maybeck was likely influenced by the color theories of Owen Jones and Gottfried Semper. Jones was superintendent of works for Joseph Paxton's Crystal Palace in London, and in his 1858 Crystal Palace Bazaar he created a chromatic glow that infused the space through implementation of stained glass triangles of red, yellow, and blue on the ceiling, his color choices based on Field's harmonic proportions.[112]

Likewise, Semper believed the ancient Greeks used color to create mood and atmosphere, such that building and environment became unified. As the architectural historian David Van Zanten wrote, "Semper and Jones imagined that a brilliantly enameled or gilded Greek temple when seen on its acropolis in the intense Mediterranean sun would simply have disappeared into some sort of vibrant 'bloom,' precisely resembling the appearance of a fine day in an Eastern climate ... Sparkling in the rising or setting sun, it would have reflected the rays and become itself a sunrise or sunset: an analogy for these great natural phenomena ... [Semper] imagined a harmony between the temple's colouring and the particular atmospheric quality of the environment." Jones and Semper believed that through the proper application of color, a building could create or recreate an entire atmosphere

FIGURE 63

FIRST CHURCH OF CHRIST, SCIENTIST, BERKELEY.

PLANTING ALONG THE WESTERN FACADE.

[MARC TREIB]

or environment, and that the color choice should respond to the setting but also to the "cultural maturity of the society producing it." The "bloom" would take on the characteristic of the place or environment "just as a flower revealed its particular nature depending on the environment in which it grew." For Jones, color in architecture was "a glowing aura expressive of the cultural soil in which the structure had grown and in grand harmony with the light and air of its surroundings."[113]

These theories neatly paralleled Maybeck's approach to the use of color. At his First Church of Christ, Scientist, he created a lighting scheme based on a subtle purple or lavender glow, intended to wash through portions of the structure, perhaps complementing certain gilded surfaces. To achieve this effect, he placed small red and blue light bulbs together in discreet locations, infusing the space with the same kind of chromatic glow that Jones aimed for in his Crystal Palace bazaar.

The Christian Science church, like the Leon Roos house, is another of Maybeck's "total designs." In addition to the church building, Maybeck designed its furnishings, light fixtures, signage, and collection bags, and, of course, a landscape.[114] Much of his plan for the grounds remains intact, though the bougainvillea, roses, hollyhocks, and hydrangeas no longer exist. Nonetheless, the landscape design for the church is remarkable in several respects, especially for its contribution to the building's color scheme.[115]

First, the site itself is quite small. The area for planting amounts to a strip only 4 or 5 feet wide between the church and the sidewalk. The southwestern corner of the lot—the location of the redwood steeple—is the exception, being larger and more open. Within this narrow space, Maybeck designed raised beds along the western elevation that increased in height at two different levels. Stepping away from the building in varying widths, the beds broaden the visual dimensions of the strip [figure 63]. The wisteria that grows vigorously on the numerous trellises and pergolas extending from the church structure is certainly the most distinguished aspect of this landscape design, though as mentioned above, wisteria was originally specified only for the church's main pergola. But the vine also serves as an important part of the interior lighting scheme: the glazing of the industrial sash windows has a lavender tint so when the wisteria is in bloom, sunlight passing through the blossoms heightens the overall purple lighting within the church. The translucent windows in the church do not eliminate a view of the foliage outside but rather diffuse leaves and flowers into a play of changing colors, light, and pattern—creating, in effect, an abstracted stained glass window. This is particularly true on the western facade, where the vine grows most heavily over the main window with its gothic-style tracery, reducing afternoon glare and heat gain inside the church.

The wisteria also contributes to the purple and pink color scheme for the planting plan. Maybeck seems to have preferred these colors as complements to the natural and stained woods of his buildings. The church landscape included wisteria, purple lantana, pink-flowering *Leptospermum* species, *Syzgium paniculatum* (brush cherry) with its purple berries, and pink roses and geraniums. The latter, in fact, was one of the architect's favored flowers, according to Jacomena Maybeck, who also remembers that "Ben [as family members and close friends referred to Maybeck] would plant Redwoods and rows of Buckeye trees in the neighborhood and collected wildflower seeds to plant during his walks in the hills."[116] This, in addition to planting designs such as the one for the Fagan residence, indicates a fondness for native species as well, closely following Keeler's approach to gardens.

The original planting plan for the church also called for *Clematis montana*, which has white blossoms that turn pink after opening, and pink Cherokee roses as climbing vines on the eastern pergolas. The main pergola was to support a combination of wisteria, bougainvillea, and pink Cherokee rose. For the raised beds, Maybeck specified pink verbena borders and solid banks of pink geraniums. Behind the boxes, centrally placed hollyhocks with pink Cherokee roses and pink blooming *Erica persoluta* acted as anchors. He placed Italian cypress directly in the center of the central raised bed in front of the main western window and surrounded these with hydrangeas. Among this riot of late winter and early spring bloom, the dark green cypress would have been the single clear focus.

Much of the original design no longer exists, although the garden remains mostly pink and purple. Rhaphiolepis, azaleas, lantana, and brush cherry now bloom instead of the roses, bougainvillea, verbena, and geraniums. Despite the changes over time, the structure and concept remain intact. The green foundation thrives, the redwood steeple gains in stature each year, and the luxuriant wisteria blooms in spring to create new and changing stained-glass windows [see figure 59].

A similar approach directed Maybeck's designs of 1935–37 for the Ninth Church of Christ, Scientist in San Francisco. Renderings for the project indicate the architect's obvious affection for masses of bloom as well as a solid understanding of appropriate groupings of annuals according to combinations of form and color. These drawings are also quite striking—rendered in brilliant, flat gouache on brown paper—and they are exuberantly covered with depictions of vegetation. Planting predominates, often occupying the primary focus of the page, nearly concealing the architecture.

Maybeck carefully composed the scheme with detailed and identifiable shrubs, trees, flowers, and vines. The rendering of the entrance depicts a garden, with little architecture shown [figures 64A, 64]. The drawing restates Maybeck's affection for the English perennial border: the flowers border a lawn and increase in height toward the enclosing wall. The rendering also invites comparison with the paintings of William Keith and Arthur Mathews. The oak in the background owes a debt to Keith as does the delicacy of the pointillist flower border, while the brilliant use of color recalls the work of Mathews.

FIGURE 64A

NINTH CHURCH OF CHRIST, SCIENTIST, SAN FRANCISCO, 1935–37 (UNBUILT).

VIEW OF ENTRANCE (DETAIL)

[EDA, UCB]

FIGURE 64

NINTH CHURCH OF CHRIST, SCIENTIST, SAN FRANCISCO, 1935–37 (UNBUILT).

VIEW OF ENTRANCE.

[EDA, UCB]

FIGURE 65

NINTH CHURCH OF CHRIST, SCIENTIST, SAN FRANCISCO, 1935–37 (UNBUILT).
RENDERING, SIDE VIEW OF SUNDAY SCHOOL.
A DOUBLE LAYER OF CLIPPED HEDGE AND WISTERIA FRONTS PURPLE-TINGED WINDOWS.
[EDA, UCB]

FIGURE 66

NINTH CHURCH OF CHRIST, SCIENTIST, SAN FRANCISCO, 1935–37 (UNBUILT). SECTION THROUGH ASSEMBLY HALL FACING SOUTH.

IN THIS DRAWING, THE RAISED BLINDS REVEAL THE PLANTING OUTSIDE THE WINDOWS.

[EDA, UCB]

The rendering labeled "Side View of Sunday School" depicts two hedge layers that provide the verdant base connecting building to site, with the second layer gaining in height closer to the building [figure 65]. Also visible in this exterior elevation are windows that Maybeck painted the same shade of purple as the wisteria blossoms delineated in front of the panes, using the planting to enforce his colored lighting scheme in shades of purple, as he did so successfully in the Berkeley Christian Science church.

In each of the interior sections, Maybeck carefully rendered the vegetation that would be viewed behind his signature use of industrial sash windows, making clear that the planting would be a part of the building's decorative embellishment [figure 66]. The landscape for this project was quite important to Maybeck. In a letter to church officials, he wrote that they should be certain to "include an item of cost to cover landscaping and planting" when formulating their budget, and he asked that any disturbed topsoil be "put aside to be used on the garden."[117] Nevertheless, the architect's drawings and careful instructions were to no avail, and his design for a second church surrounded by a luxuriant and colorful garden remained unrealized.

Kenneth Cardwell noted that Maybeck used very little color on his buildings in his first ten years of work, relying instead on the landscape to provide the chromatic interest.[118] This remained true long after his initial decade of practice had passed. For example, the architect envisioned walls of flowers for his Principia campus design, which were to be supported on wire, creating cascades of color.[119] Moreover, his drawings for the Western Hills Cemetery, designed in collaboration with Julia Morgan in 1940, employed color in large-scale planting design to dramatic effect, at least as depicted in the drawings [figure 67A, 67].

FIGURE 67A

WESTERN HILLS CEMETERY, LAWNDALE, 1940.
BERNARD MAYBECK AND JULIA MORGAN.
PERSPECTIVE (DETAIL).
[EDA, UCB]

FIGURE 67

WESTERN HILLS CEMETERY, LAWNDALE, 1940.
BERNARD MAYBECK AND JULIA MORGAN.
PERSPECTIVE.
[EDA, UCB]

WATER (AND COLOR)

Maybeck included water in his designs primarily for large-scale public projects. Although few of these were ever realized, his drawings attest to an affinity for water used to reflect landscape and color. This was crucial to his scheme for the Oakland Packard showroom, as mentioned previously, where the building's reflection in Lake Merritt determined the final exterior color scheme. But Maybeck also used water as grandiose civic embellishment and as another means for weaving together landscape and architecture.

The Palace of Fine Arts demonstrated the architect's ability to manipulate water and light in the landscape, as well as his talent for integrating planting and architecture. William Jordy called the palace "a magnificent, immense garden structure."[120] Indeed, Maybeck's original sketch of the Palace of Fine Arts reveals his desire for a structure intimately connected with and reflected in the waters of the adjacent lagoon [figure 68]. His inscription on the study reads "Palace of Fine Arts without the trimmings—this the main hall." While the drawing probably indicates one of the exhibition halls rather than Maybeck's colonnaded structure, it exposes his original conceptual intent of the play of color against the surrounding sky, water, and vegetation. Among Maybeck's office records for the Palace of Fine Arts is a letter he wrote stating that "on the whole the lagoon is the crux of the whole composition," a point made evident by the conceptual drawing.[121] Additionally, the radius of the colonnade that curves around the lagoon is struck not from the center of the rotunda, as one would expect, but rather from a point in the middle of the lagoon, further strengthening the relation of the structure to the water because the geometry for the site originates in the landscape rather than the architecture.[122]

The lagoon's irregular manner and plantings contrasted sharply with the more geometrically formal landscape treatment used throughout the fair, though as mentioned previously, Maybeck's green terraces rising from the lagoon resonated with John McLaren's green southern wall. Donald McLaren (the assistant chief of the Department of Landscape Gardening at the exposition) characterized Maybeck's work as "A very fine example of the natural treatment, provided by the architect in connection with the planting up of the lagoon in front of the Fine Arts Building."[123] Mullgardt also described the design in these terms, stating that "the landscape, in its simple naturalness, is in feeling an intimate part of the building itself and so perfectly do they blend that they seem to have grown together through quiet, serene centuries."[124] This quality of age was very important to Maybeck. It was difficult to achieve with new plantings but, as Cardwell noted, Maybeck "connived with his friend McLaren to drop several truckloads of large trees destined for other areas into the muck surrounding the lagoon... When he came to have them removed to their assigned destinations, the trees had sunk far enough into the mire to make it impossible."[125] By using these waylaid trees, Maybeck could create the appearance of mature plantings through mass, if not through trunk girth and tree height.

FIGURE 68

PALACE OF FINE ARTS, SAN FRANCISCO, CIRCA 1914. CONCEPTUAL STUDY.

[EDA, UCB]

Showing his understanding of the dynamic, temporal aspects of landscape design and his desire that the structure should acquire the mood of a Piranesian ruin as planting overtook the structure in time, Maybeck wrote,

> *It was intended that the foliage should be high and romantic avoiding all stiff lines, but the scale being so large it was impossible to plant things large enough and with restricted means and time to realize the intention. If it were a permanent building, the planting could be arranged to have the proper mass in ten to twenty years or more.*[126]

In many respects (and despite his disappointment over the loss of planting in the boxes high above the colonnade), the palace was a great success. The project brought Maybeck a considerable amount of recognition both within the architectural profession and among the public, greatly enhancing his career. So successful was this monument in the eyes of the public that, long after the exposition had ended, funds were raised for its reconstruction in permanent materials. Thanks to those efforts, the rotunda and colonnade stand today as a powerful example of Maybeck's Mediterranean garden-architecture aesthetic. His use of color recalls Pompeii: the Tuscan red and ocher reverberate against the sky and reflect off the water in the lagoon [figure 69]. While these colors were compatible with Jules Guérin's comprehensive color scheme for the exposition, Maybeck's architectural contribution was quite distinctive. As Louis Christian Mullgardt stated, "The entire composition bespeaks the mind of a romanticist, whose productions are swayed more by nature's glories than by scholastic tradition."[127] The Palace of Fine Arts was certainly one of Maybeck's most romantic creations. It conveyed the qualities of the region through its site plan and design rather than merely storing and displaying the products of California in a decorated warehouse.

Around 1922 another opportunity for a grand-scale public project appeared across the bay, at the University of California. Following his mother's death in 1919, William Randolph Hearst initiated a competition for a memorial to Phoebe Apperson

FIGURE 69 *(opposite)*

PALACE OF FINE ARTS, SAN FRANCISCO, REFLECTED IN THE LAGOON, CIRCA 1915. HAND-COLORED PHOTOGRAPH.

[THAT WAS A DREAM WORTH BUILDING]

MEMORIAL
TO
PHOEBE A HEAR
WILLIAM RANDOLPH HE
DONOR

FIGURE 70

PHOEBE APPERSON HEARST MEMORIAL, UNIVERSITY OF CALIFORNIA, BERKELEY, 1928. RENDERING.

[EDA, UCB]

Hearst, one of the greatest benefactors of the Berkeley campus, and Maybeck entered several remarkable drawings. Although the architectural program was vague, Maybeck designed a series of elaborate domed and vaulted alternatives that could have incorporated auditorium, gymnasium, and museums. The site for the Phoebe Hearst memorial was in the vicinity of the current Hearst gymnasium but somewhat to the north and incorporated Strawberry Creek. The memorial was never built owing to diversion of funds for other campus building projects of greater priority to both the university and the donor.[128] But the pastel renderings Maybeck produced to illustrate its design reveal an elaborate landscape scheme developed in conjunction with the architecture of the memorial. Enormous vaulted structures were surrounded by elaborate watercourses and raised beds that were heavily planted [figure 70]. Vines crept down the walls that contained the planted areas and the vegetation pressed in on the vaulted structure. In a loosely sketched plan, water ran directly through the architecture, again blurring the distinction between figure and ground [figure 71].

Like the Palace of Fine Arts, the water and planting created a framework for the architecture. Perhaps Maybeck's design for the Hearst memorial was, as Gray Brechin has postulated, to "have been a small scale re-creation, in permanent materials, of the Pan Pacific International Exposition, with polychrome classical buildings and detached architectural groupings resembling ruins enclosing a series of sheltered courts."[129] Certainly, the designs recall the Palace of Fine Arts, but even more characteristic is the use of water for reflection, of planting to fill out the composition of the ground plan, and of architecture and landscape inextricably linked [figure 72]. The rendering of the memorial, with its open air design and hybrid classicism, alludes to Roman baths, recalling again the Mediterranean analogy. Sunlight washes through the drawing, across the architecture, planting, and water to create the warm glow of an idealized California, the Athens of the West.

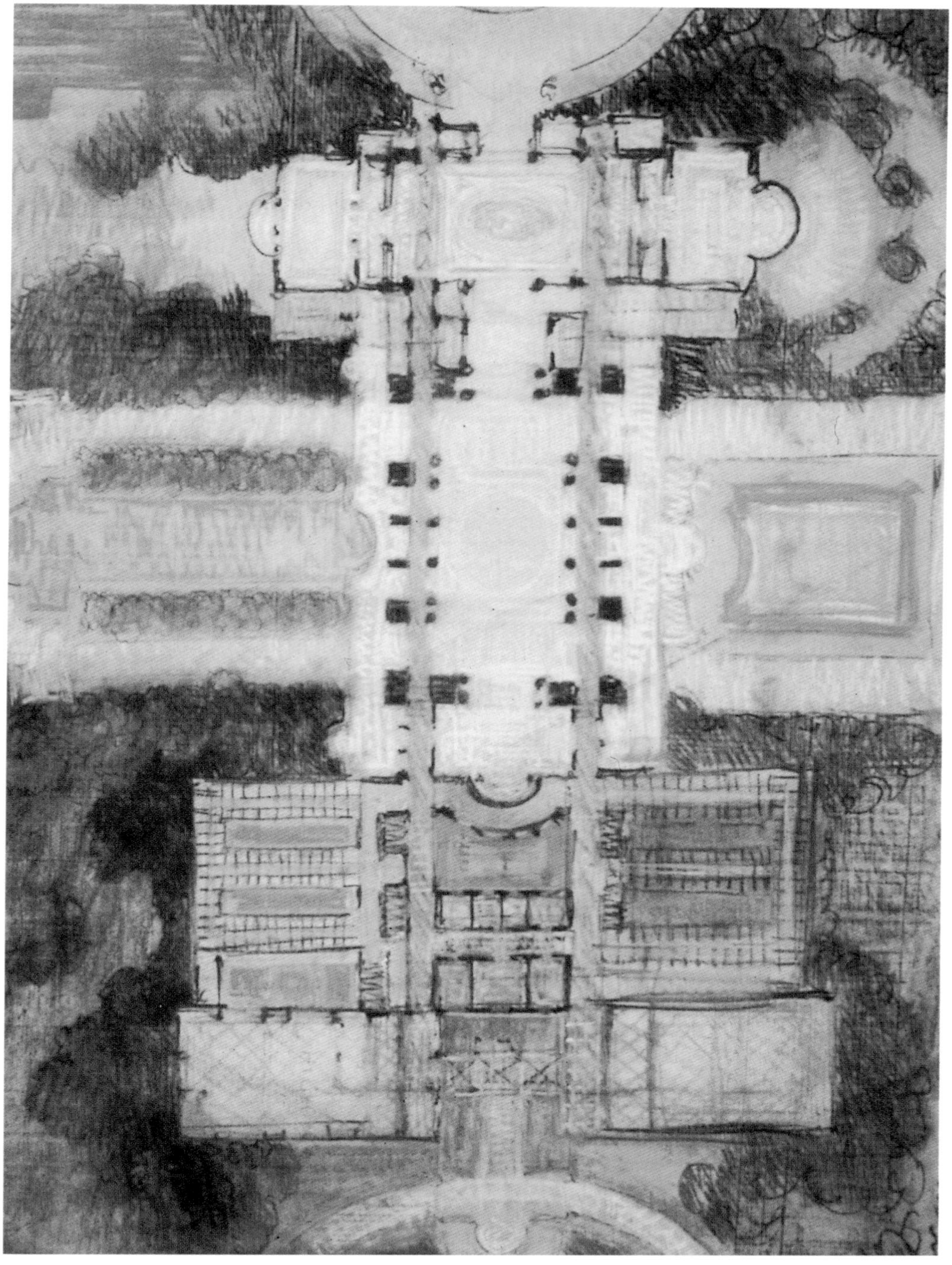

FIGURE 71

PHOEBE APPERSON HEARST MEMORIAL, UNIVERSITY OF CALIFORNIA, BERKELEY, 1928. SKETCH PLAN.
TWO PARALLEL BLUE BANDS INDICATE WATER THAT WAS TO FLOW BOTH INSIDE AND OUTSIDE THE STRUCTURE.
[EDA, UCB]

FIGURE 72

PHOEBE HEARST MEMORIAL, CIRCA 1923.
PERSPECTIVE.
[EDA, UCB]

Finally, Maybeck's unbuilt designs for a series of cascades on Twin Peaks in San Francisco (no date, but probably made after 1930) display an exuberant use of water and landscape elements. The project includes four magnificent and unusually large drawings, each approximately 3 feet wide and nearly 6 feet long, rendered freehand in colored chalk on brown paper [figures 73A, 73, 74A, 74]. Additional drawings depicted an auditorium on Twin Peaks and parks that linked the cascades to the city's neighborhoods, which were bisected by broad, curving, tree-lined streets, making the entire eastern end of San Francisco appear to be a unified irregular-form park. Like Maybeck's design proposal for the Berkeley harbor—with its grand axes, large areas of water, and abundant greenery—the Twin Peaks renderings were not commissioned but were instead visionary proposals created without a client [figure 75].[130] In both cases, the exact intention is not entirely clear, but both projects tell of the architect's desire to create urban landscapes that would foster strong civic identities.

Though no additional information exists in Maybeck's office files for the Twin Peaks drawings, the designs appear to derive from Daniel Burnham's *Plan for San Francisco* of 1904. Burnham was invited by the city to create a comprehensive plan for San Francisco, as he had for Washington, Cleveland, Chicago, and Manila.[131] Burnham agreed to do the work without a fee but requested a bungalow be constructed for his living quarters and studio on Twin Peaks, where he could have a commanding view of the city. The 1904 plan was widely publicized, and Maybeck would certainly have known its contents, including the Burnham design for Twin Peaks.

Burnham's scheme included a series of hilltop parks encircling the city, and Twin Peaks produced the visual terminus to Market and Mission streets. He wrote that it should be "marked by terraces leading the eye to the summit."[132] Burnham envisioned these terraces occupied by various features that together would form a magnificent public festival ground, becoming the physical and cultural center of the city. The

FIGURE 73A

TWIN PEAKS CASCADES, NO DATE (UNBUILT). (DETAIL)

[EDA, UCB]

FIGURE 73 (*opposite*)

TWIN PEAKS CASCADES, NO DATE (UNBUILT).

[EDA, UCB]

FIGURE 74A
TWIN PEAKS CASCADES, NO DATE (UNBUILT). (DETAIL)
[EDA, UCB]

FIGURE 74 *(opposite)*
TWIN PEAKS CASCADES, NO DATE (UNBUILT).
AN ALTERNATE SCHEME.
[EDA, UCB]

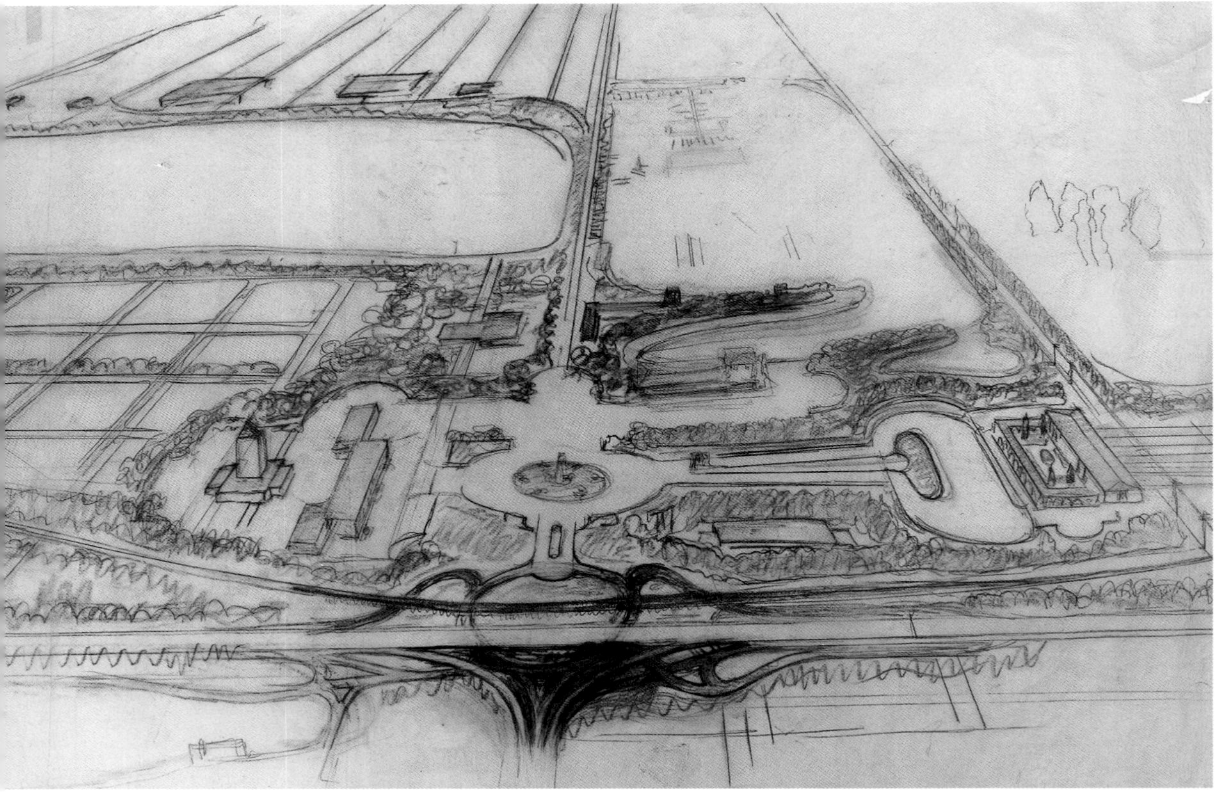

FIGURE 75

DESIGN FOR BERKELEY HARBOR, BERKELEY, NO DATE.

[EDA, UCB]

features included an amphitheater or stadium "of vast proportions" that would recall Delphi, an academy based on a Greek model for the accommodation of "men of intellectual and artistic pursuits," and an athenaeum designed in the manner of the Great Poecile at Hadrian's Villa, intended for the display of great works of art [figure 76].

Burnham's plan integrated the city's water supply system into the Twin Peaks scheme. He wrote,

> *The water supply of San Francisco will eventually be obtained from the Sierras. As it will be limitless, the reservoirs should be vast and designed to be in themselves a feature of the city. They should be placed at such a height that the water may be used for fire purposes, fountains and water works of all descriptions.*
>
> *At some extra cost a superb effect might be produced by using a number of reservoirs at successive heights. The water, arriving at the highest point through a triumphal entrance, would fall from one level to another in cascades, thus producing a veritable "Chateau d'Eau." These reservoirs at different levels would supply corresponding heights in the city and the water would be aerated by means of the cascades. The main reservoir should be placed at the western foot of Twin Peaks.*[133]

In all likelihood, Burnham's plans were instigation for Maybeck's design for the Twin Peaks cascades. In fact, the drawings appear to be direct and fairly literal translations of Burnham's prescribed treatment. Maybeck designed two distinctly different versions of his cascades: one is rugged and irregular, the other a Beaux-Arts fantasy complete with Burnham's suggested Greek and Roman allusions. A third drawing represents the classical design as it would have appeared at night with special lighting effects playing off the temple-like structures and the cascading water. The project indicates an interest in manipulating landscape, water, and light to create a monumental civic focal point.

FIGURE 76

"APPROACH TO TWIN PEAKS AS SEEN FROM MARKET STREET." DANIEL BURNHAM.

[REPORT ON A PLAN FOR SAN FRANCISCO]

The Twin Peaks drawings may also have been partially inspired by Maybeck's friend Charles Keeler. Toward the end of his life, Keeler wrote of his wishes for a temple in the hills for his "cosmic religion." He wrote, "within such a temple would be the magic of modern lighting producing strangely beautiful effects falling upon moving water." Perhaps Keeler shared this design fantasy with Maybeck, resulting in the cascade designs. It is also possible that the Twin Peaks schemes were part of the architect's ideal city plan for San Francisco.[134] Whatever the impetus for their creation, the drawings are remarkable for their monumentalized portraiture of Maybeck's involvement with landscape design.

The projects presented here are only a selection of the many Maybeck completed during the course of his long career, but they serve as an indicative representation of his landscape interests. As such, they expose another dimension of the architect's design process and sensibility. Simply characterized, Maybeck combined his École des Beaux-Arts education and Parisian experiences with his knowledge of international, national, and local landscape and architectural design trends. Add to the mix a flair for innovation and his engagement with the regional culture and creative atmosphere of northern California in the early part of the century, and the result is a uniquely integrated approach to design of the built environment.

Maybeck's landscape designs create a new framework for understanding his career. To study Maybeck's architecture without his landscape designs is to ignore half of the picture. Not only does he rank among a very few early twentieth-century architects with outstanding abilities to combine building, garden, and landscape, he was also far ahead of his time; he was instrumental in developing what was later to become known—through the work of Thomas Church, William Wurster, Gardner Dailey, Garret Eckbo, and others—as the modern Californian house and garden, the model of integrated indoor-outdoor living. Maybeck was highly skilled in his creation of outdoor rooms, in connecting architecture and the garden, and in selecting plant materials appropriate to the region: all were hallmarks of the modern Californian garden.

Moreover, Maybeck's landscape approach is also exemplary for its spatial richness. He understood that the tools of the landscape architect were similar to, and sometimes equivalent with, those of the architect. They included manipulation of the ground plane, the use and arrangement of various types of vertical surfaces, and a range of canopies (both architectural and vegetative) to create degrees of enclosure. He easily deployed the dynamic qualities that are inherent to landscape design, manipulating light and seasonally variable vegetation to full effect. Unlike much recent work in the field of landscape architecture, Maybeck designed spaces that were primarily interesting in three dimensions. Because they were integrally linked to his architecture, they could not be developed as merely flat or patterned surfaces. His architectural training, with its (perhaps) old-fashioned emphasis on the study of complex geometry and spatial development, predisposed him to regard the design of all space—whether indoors or out—as a problem of three-dimensional expression. That he drew perspectives so often is therefore not surprising, since plans and elevations tell only a portion of the story.[135] Sectional studies of his projects, though rare, are all the more revealing of this quality.

Should we think of Bernard Maybeck then as a landscape architect as well? Perhaps, though not to any greater degree than we consider him an architect. After all, he clearly regarded the two as constituent parts of a greater whole. As Maybeck wrote in an essay on his work at Principia College, "For want of a better word, 'architecture' is often used in the sense of that peculiar physiognomy of the surface of forms: facades of churches, temples, palaces, tombs and even gardens."[136] Especially gardens.

NOTES

1. Dianne Harris, "Architecture and the Garden: The Landscape Designs of Bernard Maybeck," master's thesis, University of California, Berkeley, 1989.

2. David Streatfield noted this as well in his *California Gardens: Creating a New Eden*, New York: Abbeville Press, 1994, pp. 8, 9.

3. Although a complete bibliography of the scholarship on landscape architecture in the United States since 1900 lies outside the scope of this study, the following recently published sources provide valuable background for placing Maybeck's work in context. In addition to David Streatfield's book, see Charles E. Aguar and Berdeana Aguar, *Wrightscapes: Frank Lloyd Wright's Landscape Designs*, New York: McGraw Hill, 2002; Robert Grese, *Jens Jensen: Maker of Natural Parks and Gardens*, Baltimore: Johns Hopkins University Press, 1992; Dennis Domer, ed., *Alfred Caldwell: The Life and Work of a Prairie School Landscape Architect*, Baltimore: Johns Hopkins University Press, 1997; William Tishler, ed., *Midwestern Landscape Architecture*, Urbana: University of Illinois Press, 2000; Therese O'Malley and Marc Treib, eds., *Regional Garden Design in the United States*, Washington, D. C.: Dumbarton Oaks, 1995; Christopher Vernon, "Walter Burley Griffin, Landscape Architect," in Crese and Garner, eds., *The Midwest in American Architecture*, Urbana: University of Illinois Press, 1991, pp. 217–30; Anne Whiston Spirn, "Frank Lloyd Wright: Architect of Landscape," in *Frank Lloyd Wright: Designs for an American Landscape, 1922–32*, New York: Harry Abrams, 1996; Jan Roberts, ed., *Avalon: Landscape and Harmony, Walter Burley Griffin, Alexander Stewart Jolly, and Harry Ruskin Stowe*, Avalon Beach: Ruskin Rowe Press, 1999; David Gebhard, *Lutah Maria Riggs: A Woman in California Architecture*, Santa Barbara: Capra Press, 1992; Charles A. Birnbaum and Robin Karson, eds., *Pioneers of American Landscape Design*, New York: McGraw Hill, 2000. There are many more titles, but these provide a starting point.

4. For more on this approach, see my introductory essay, "Landscape in Context," in Mirka Benes and Dianne Harris, eds., *Villas and Gardens in Early Modern Italy and France*, New York: Cambridge University Press, 2001, pp. 16–28.

5. See Kenneth Cardwell, *Bernard Maybeck: Artisan, Architect, Artist*, Salt Lake City: Peregrine Smith Books, 1977; Richard Longstreth, *On the Edge of the World: Four Architects in San Francisco at the Turn of the Century*, Cambridge, Mass.: Architectural History Foundation and MIT Press, 1983; William H. Jordy, *American Buildings and Their Architects: Progressive and Academic Ideals at the Turn of the Twentieth Century*, Oxford: Oxford University Press, 1972; Sally Woodbridge, *Bernard Maybeck: Visionary Architect*,

New York: Abbeville Press, 1992. There are many additional studies, but these remain at the core of the scholarship on Maybeck.

6. For more detailed information on the Bernard Maybeck collection, see the online catalog of the Environmental Design Archives of the University of California, Berkeley (hereafter EDA, UCB), www.ced.berkeley.edu/cedarchives/use.html; and the Online Archive of California, http://findaid.oac.cdlib.org/findaid/ark:/13030/, and follow links to the Maybeck Collection. The latter has a link with detailed information about the archive's Maybeck holdings, which include personal papers, correspondence, office files, project files, drawings, and photographs.

7. *Hillside Club Yearbook, 1906–07*, The Bancroft Library, University of California, Berkeley. See also Dimitri Shipounoff, introduction to *The Simple Home*, by Charles Keeler, Santa Barbara: Peregrine Smith, 1979, p. xi.

8. The first published studies on Maybeck's landscapes were my own (see "Maybeck's Landscapes," *Journal of Garden History*, 1989; and "Making Gardens in the Athens of the West: Bernard Maybeck and the San Francisco Bay Region Tradition in Landscape and Garden Design," in O'Malley and Treib, *Regional Garden Design*, pp. 43–68).

9. For example, Sally Woodbridge noted that landscape design was important to Maybeck but added that "almost no evidence remains of his intentions for the landscaping of his buildings" (Woodbridge, *Bernard Maybeck*, pp. 11–12). Woodbridge, like many architectural historians, likely overlooked the significance of the landscape rendered on the majority of his drawings, perhaps dismissing it as typical "entourage."

10. See the sources cited in note 3.

11. Robert Judson Clarke has argued that the analogy is more correctly associated with Rome, since the architectural model tended to be Italy more frequently than Greece. His "Roma Pacifica" stands as a corrective to what he has called the "misnomer 'Athens of the West.'" Robert Judson Clarke, lecture at the School of Architecture, University of Illinois, Urbana-Champaign, November 19, 2002. However, documents and evidence connecting the analogy to Greece remain numerous. See for example, Gray Brechin, *Imperial San Francisco: Urban Power, Earthly Ruin*, Berkeley: University of California Press, 1999, pp. 285–89.

12. Bernard Maybeck, "Regional Architecture," Mills College job file, manuscript dated 1918, pp. 6–7. Maybeck Collection EDA, UCB.

13. The fact that the Mediterranean metaphor has endured in California for so long and has prevailed with such currency owes something to both governmental and corporate power structures that stood to profit from the rapid settlement and large-scale agricultural development of the state, achieved through proliferation of the myth. For more on this, see Donald Worster, *Rivers of Empire: Water, Aridity, and the Growth of the American West*, New York: Oxford University Press, 1985; William Alexander McClung, *Landscapes of Desire: Anglo Mythologies of Los Angeles*, Berkeley: University of California Press, 2000.

14. Kevin Starr, *Americans and the California Dream*, Salt Lake City: Peregrine Smith, 1981, pp. 366, 370, 367, 369. Starr gives no source for this information, but Olmsted's involvement as manager of the Mariposa Mining estate is well documented elsewhere, as is his relationship to Fremont. See Victoria Post Ranney, ed., *The Papers of Frederick Law Olmsted, vol. 5, The California Frontier, 1863–65*, Baltimore: Johns Hopkins University Press, 1990, ch. 4.

15. Ranney, *Papers of Olmsted, vol. 5*, pp. 110, 111.

16. Ibid., p. 105, letter from Olmsted to wife dated October 1863; pp. 451 and, on Olmsted's designs for Stanford, 458. See also Olmsted's essay, "Notes on the Pioneer Condition," published in the same volume.

17. According to Kenneth Cardwell, Maybeck was responsible for Guadet's later involvement in the development of the building programs for the Berkeley campus competition, and he collaborated

with him on that assignment. Cardwell, *Maybeck*, pp. 42, 43.

18. Ibid., p. 90. Cardwell asserts that Maybeck read Semper's *Der Stil* but the architect's knowledge of polychromy could have derived from a number of published sources in currency at the end of the nineteenth century.

19. Annie Jacques, "The Programmes of the Architectural Section of the École des Beaux-Arts, 1819–1914," in Robin Middleton, ed., *The Beaux-Arts and Nineteenth-Century French Architecture*, Cambridge: MIT Press, 1982, p. 61.

20. Jacques, "Programmes of the Architectural Section," pp. 62, 65; on Guillaume, see p. 65.

21. Warren Perry's drawings are located in The Bancroft Library, University of California, Berkeley. For Chifflot's drawing see David van Zanten, "Architectural Composition at the École des Beaux-Arts," in Arthur Drexler, ed., *The Architecture of the École des Beaux-Arts*, New York: Museum of Modern Art and Cambridge, Mass.: MIT Press, 1977, p. 320

22. Cardwell, *Maybeck*, p. 18.

23. Leslie Mandelson Freudenheim and Elisabeth Sussman, *Building with Nature: Roots of the San Francisco Bay Region Tradition*, Santa Barbara: Peregrine Smith, 1974, pp. 45, 69.

24. Dorothée Imbert, *The Modernist Garden in France*, New Haven: Yale University Press, 1993, pp. x, xi.

25. See Édouard André, *L'art des jardins: traité général de la composition des parcs et jardins* (1879); reprint, Marseille: Laffitte, 1983.

27. Imbert, *Modernist Garden*, pp. 3, 11.

28. David Van Zanten, "Architectural Composition," in Drexler, ed., *École des Beaux-Arts*, pp. 111–324.

28. Neil Levine, "The Romantic Idea of Architectural Legibility: Henri Labrouste and the Neo-Grec," in ibid., pp. 338, 347.

29. Neil Levine, "The Book and the Building: Hugo's Theory of architecture and Labrouste's Bibliothèque Ste-Geneviève," in Middleton, *The Beaux-Arts and Nineteenth-Century French Architecture*, p. 161.

30. Levine, "Romantic Idea," p. 403; see also his "Book and the Building," p. 139.

31. David Van Zanten, "Architectural Composition," in Drexler, ed., *École des Beaux-Arts*, p. 290. Bénard became the winner of the Phoebe Hearst competition for a plan for the Berkeley campus in 1899.

32. Starr, *California Dream*, p. 425. Luther Burbank, for example, who came to California in 1875 and earned a reputation as a talented nurseryman and hybridizer was, like so many others of his time, self-taught; see also p. 430.

33. Deborah Nevins, "Morris, Ruskin and the English Flower Garden," *Antiques*, June 1986, p. 1257. See also Reginald Blomfield and Inigo F. Thomas, *The Formal Garden in England*, London: Macmillan, 1892, as well as its 1901 3rd ed.; John Sedding, *Garden-Craft Old and New*, London: K. Paul, Trench, Trübner, 1892; William Robinson, *The Wild Garden, or Our Groves & Shrubberies Made Beautiful*, London: John Murray, 1870. For a scholarly treatment of English trends and the Blomfield/Robinson debate, see Anne Helmreich, *The English Garden and National Identity: The Competing Styles of Garden Design, 1870–1914*, New York: Cambridge University Press, 2002; on Arts and Crafts gardens see Wendy Hitchmough, *Arts and Crafts Gardens*, New York: Rizzoli, 1997; for their influence in California, see Streatfield, *California Gardens*, ch. 3. There are numerous studies of Gertrude Jekyll; a fine treatment is Jane Brown, *Gardens of a Golden Afternoon*, New York: Penguin Books, 1982. See also Sally Festing, *Gertrude Jekyll*, London: Penguin Books, 1991.

34. Robinson, *The Wild Garden*.

35. On Charles Platt, see his *Italian Gardens*, 1898; reprint, Portland, Ore.: Saga/Timber Press, 1993; Keith Morgan, *Charles A.*

Platt: The Artist as Architect, New York: Architectural History Foundation and MIT Press, 1985. On Wilson Eyre and Frank Miles Day, see Longstreth, *On the Edge of the World*, p. 187. Architects like Platt frequently collaborated with skilled planting designers such as Ellen Biddle Shipman. The Gwinn estate in Cleveland, Ohio, is one example. As such, their collaborations were similar to the Lutyens/ Jekyll partnership in which Edwin Lutyens created the geometric scheme for the garden's layout and Gertrude Jekyll designed the artful and informally massed plantings contained within the prescribed beds. See Robin Karson, *The Muses of Gwinn*, New York: Harry N. Abrams, 1996; Brown, *Gardens of a Golden Afternoon*. Bruce Porter collaborated on several projects with Willis Polk. He designed the gardens for the Francis Carolan estate in Burlingame Park of 1899, and the Bourn (Filoli) estate in Woodside of 1914–15. See Longstreth, *On the Edge of the World*, p. 187.

36. An avid follower of Jekyll's work, Farrand purchased Jekyll's papers after her death and integrated them into her Reef Point Library. Farrand's library and papers, along with Jekyll's, ultimately became the property of EDA, UCB.

37. See Mac Griswold and Eleanor Weller, *The Golden Age of American Gardens: Proud Owners, Private Estates, 1890–1940*, New York: Harry Abrams, 1992, p. 18.

38. Letter in Principia job file dated 9 May 24, Maybeck Collection, EDA, UCB. The archives at Principia College contain an extensive collection of Maybeck's drawings for and writings about the campus design. Included among these are numerous colored chalk drawings of landscape design, such as tree groupings and placement, and vines that were intended to grow onto building facades. These drawings can be viewed online at www.prin.edu/maybeck/arch/1932.htm. For more on Maybeck's work at Principia, see Robert M. Craig, *Bernard Maybeck at Principia College: The Art and Craft of Building*, Layton, Utah: Gibbs Smith Publishers, 2004. The architecture at Principia may be some of Maybeck's weakest; its quaint nostalgia, derived from English vernacular models, makes the buildings appear less regionally specific than his other work, yet it is also less imaginative.

39. Maybeck cited in Mark Stevens, "An Architect is Chosen," *Principia Pilot*, 19 November 1971, p. 5. On the sketch, see Ann Wheeler, "The Maybeck Challenge, The Maybeck Answer," in the same issue.

40. Letter in Principia job file addressed to Mrs. William Morgan, 1924, Maybeck Collection, EDA, UCB. See notebook entitled "General Impressions," in ibid.

41. Starr, *California Dream*, pp. 407, 408.

42. Una Nixson Hopkins, "The Development of Domestic Architecture on the Pacific Coast," *The Craftsman* 13, no.4, January 1908, p. 450. Hopkins contributed frequently to shelter magazines in the early decades of the twentieth century. In addition to being a novelist, her writings can be found in the *Ladies' Home Journal*, *House Beautiful*, and *The Craftsman*. See John William Leonard, ed., *Woman's Who's Who of America, 1914–15*, New York: American Commonwealth, 1914, p. 403.

43. In time some of these integrative design characteristics became commonplace with indoor/outdoor connections an expected aspect of most ordinary housing, especially on the West Coast. On this topic, see for example, the essays in Marc Treib, ed., *An Everyday Modernism: The Houses of William Wurster*, Berkeley: University of California Press, 1995; Dianne Harris, "Making Your Private World: Modern Landscape Architecture and *House Beautiful*, 1945–1965," in Marc Treib, ed., *The Architecture of Landscape 1940–1960*, Philadelphia: University of Pennsylvania Press, 2002, pp. 180–205; Marc Treib, "Aspects of Regionality and the Modern(ist) Garden in California," in O'Malley and Treib, eds., *Regional Garden Design*, pp. 43–68.

44. See Elizabeth C. MacPhail, *Kate Sessions: Pioneer Horticulturist*, San Diego: San Diego Historical Society, 1976. On Gill's work with Sessions see also Streatfield, *California Gardens*, 74–75; on Gill, see

Esther McCoy, *Five California Architects*, Los Angeles: Hennessey and Ingalls, 1960, pp. 59–102; Charles Gibbs Adams, "Gardens of the Stars," *Saturday Evening Post*, 2 March 1940, p. 74; Sarah Holmes Boutelle, *Julia Morgan, Architect*, New York: Abbeville, 1988.

45. John McLaren was superintendent of parks for San Francisco and for the Panama Pacific International Exposition. Although he referred to himself as a nurseryman, he was largely responsible for creating most of San Francisco's major green spaces and forestation and wrote one book, *Gardening in California: Landscape and Flower*, San Francisco: A. M. Robertson, 1908. Mark Daniels worked as both an architect and landscape architect, first as the landscape engineer for Yosemite National Park in 1914 and as general superintendent and landscape engineer for the National Parks Service until 1916. He designed subdivisions, company towns, and campus plans and served as landscape architect for the Golden Gate International Exposition in 1939–40. Carmel's 17-mile drive is among his most famous projects, which he completed with Chesley Bonestall. John William Gregg taught landscape architecture at UCB. For more on Gregg, see *John Gregg: A Half-Century of Landscape Architecture*, Berkeley: Regional Oral History Office, 1965. Aside from his work on Principia College, Butler Stevens Sturtevant practiced primarily in Seattle and the Pacific Northwest. His well-known projects include Normandy Park in Seattle and the rose garden at Butchart Gardens outside Victoria in British Columbia.

46. McCoy, *Five California Architects*, p. 83.

47. Irving Gill, "The Home of the Future, The New Architecture of the West: Small Homes for a Great Country, Number Four," *The Craftsman* 30, no. 2, May 1916, pp. 148, 145.

48. Randell Makinson, "Greene and Greene" in McCoy, *Five California Architects*, p. 137. For more on the Greene brothers' approach to landscape, see Janet Lynn Brown, "Charles Sumner and Henry Mather Greene, Architects: The Integration of House and Garden, Southern California, 1989–1914," master's thesis, University of California, Berkeley, 1988. See also Streatfield, *California Gardens*, pp. 77, 79, 83; Anne Bloomfield, "The Evolution of a Landscape: Charles Sumner Greene's Designs for Green Gables," *Journal of the Society of Architectural Historians*, September 1988, pp. 231–44; Randell Makinson, *Greene and Greene*; Henry Hawley, "An Italianate Garden by Greene and Greene," *Journal of Decorative and Propoganda Arts* 2, Summer–Fall 1986, pp. 32–45. See also McCoy, *Five California Architects*, p. 117.

49. For an important scholarly overview of Wright's career, see Neil Levine, *The Architecture of Frank Lloyd Wright*, Princeton: Princeton University Press, 1997. On Wright's approach to and understanding of landscape, see "Concerning Landscape Architecture," in Bruce Pfeiffer, ed., *Frank Lloyd Wright: Collected Writings*, New York: Rizzoli, 1992, pp. 54–57; Spirn, "Frank Lloyd Wright," in De Long, ed., *Frank Lloyd Wright*, pp. 135–69; Aguar and Aguar, *Wrightscapes*; David Van Zanten, ed., *The Nature of Frank Lloyd Wright*, Chicago: University of Chicago Press, 1988; Catherine Howett, "Frank Lloyd Wright and American Residential Landscaping," *Landscape* 26, no. 1, 1982, pp. 45–57; William Cronon, "Inconstant Unity: The Passion of Frank Lloyd Wright," in Terence Riley, ed., *Frank Lloyd Wright, Architect*, New York: Museum of Modern Art, 1994.

50. Spirn, "Architect of Landscape," in De Long, ed., *Frank Lloyd Wright*, p. 140. On Wright's use of the grid, see pp. 150–51. On his preference for native species and the retention of existing site character, see Aguar and Aguar, *Wrightscapes*, p. ix.

51. The only reference to Wright I have found among Maybeck's papers appears in the project file for Principia College in a letter from Darwin D. Martin to Frederic E. Morgan, 5 Sep 1930, offering the services of his architect, Frank Lloyd Wright, for the design of the campus buildings. When Morgan wrote to ask Maybeck if he knew of Wright's work, he replied affirmatively, but without further comment.

52. Spirn, "Architect of Landscape," in De Long, ed., *Frank Lloyd Wright*, p. 158.

53. Longstreth, *On the Edge of the World*, pp. 121, 127, 185.

54. See Robert Judson Clark, "Louis Christian Mullgardt," in Robert W. Winter, ed., *Toward a Simpler Way of Life: The Arts and Crafts Architects of California*, Berkeley: University of California Press, 1997, pp. 46–47.

55. For more on some of the personalities involved, see Birgitta Hjalmarson, *Artful Players: Artistic Life in Early San Francisco*, New York: Princeton Architectural Press, 2001.

56. Shipounoff, introduction, pp. xxxi, xi. Keeler was a prolific author. A sampling of his other publications indicates his interest in writing both natural history and booster texts: *Sequoia Sonnets* (1919); *Bird Notes Afield* (1907); *San Francisco and Thereabout* (1902); *To California and Back, a Book of Practical Information for Travelers to the Pacific* (1903); *San Francisco through Earthquake and Fire* (1906).

57. Keeler, *Simple Home*, pp. 12–13.

58. Ibid., pp. 11, 13–14.

59. Ibid., pp. 14–15.

60. Shipounoff, introduction, p. xxvii.

61. Jordy, *American Buildings*, p. 284.

62. Werner Hegemann, *Report on a City Plan for the Municipalities of Oakland and Berkeley*, Oakland and Berkeley: Municipal Governments of Oakland and Berkeley, 1915, pp. 114–15. With Elbert Peets, Hegemann authored *American Vitruvius: An Architect's Handbook of Civic Art*, New York: Architectural Book Publishing, 1922.

63. McCoy, *Five California Architects*, p. 57.

64. Cardwell, *Maybeck*, p. 189.

65. In general, Maybeck was quite interested in new materials and technologies of all sorts. His papers include sketches for the design of an airplane, but he also created an innovative form of concrete called "bubblestone" and experimented with tilt-up, prefabricated concrete walls in the Lawson House, Berkeley, 1907.

66. Worcester's description of his Piedmont garden illustrates the scene encountered by Maybeck when he approached his neighbor's house. Worcester wrote, "I have been setting out vines about the house this week, climbing roses, passion vines, begonias, etc. and at a little distance I have set out currant and gooseberry bushes and apple, pear and cherry trees." Freudenheim and Sussmann, *Building with Nature*, p. 10. For more on Worcester's house, and on his relationship to Maybeck, William Keith, and others, see Longstreth, *On the Edge of the World*, pp. 111–17 and 74. For more on the Arts and Crafts movement in California, see Streatfield, *California Gardens*; Hitchmough, *Arts and Crafts Gardens*; and Helmreich, *English Garden and National Identity*.

67. Charles Keeler, "Friends Bearing Torches," p. 226, cited in Shipounoff, introduction, p. xix. "Friends Bearing Torches" was a collection of biographical essays on California luminaries such as Worcester, Keith, and Charles Fletcher Lummis.

68. Edward R. Bosley, "A. C. Schweinfurth," in Winter, ed., *Toward a Simpler Way of Life*, p. 12.

69. Longstreth, *On the Edge of the World*, pp. 273–75.

70. Freudenheim and Sussmann, *Building with Nature*, p. 25.

71. Eugen Neuhaus, *William Keith: The Man and the Artist*, Berkeley: University of California Press, 1938, p. 66.

72. Ibid., p. 24.

73. Ibid.

74. Brother Fidelis Cornelius, *Keith, Old Master of California*, New York: G. P. Putnam's Sons, 1942, p. 234.

75. Neuhaus, *William Keith*, pp. 48, 71.

76. On this project, see Earle C. Anthony, *The Romance of Transportation in California and Story of the Packard Building*, Oakland, 1928. My thanks to Richard

Longstreth for directing me to this publication.

77. Van Zanten, "Architectural Polychromy: Life in Architecture," in Middleton, ed., *Beaux-Arts*, p. 211.

78. The literature on the picturesque related to garden theory is vast, but for an introduction to the key ideas from the perspective of aesthetic and literary theory, see two works by John Dixon Hunt, *The Picturesque Garden in Europe*, London: Thames and Hudson, 2002; and *Gardens and the Picturesque: Studies in the History of Landscape Architecture*, Cambridge, Mass.: MIT Press, 1992; as well as John Dixon Hunt and Peter Willis, eds., *The Genius of the Place: The English Landscape Garden, 1620–1820*, New York: Harper, 1975.

79. See Senger job file, Maybeck Collection. George Hansen served as landscape consultant on the Senger residence. His notes indicate the importance of the redwood trees as a framing device and threshold for the garden and site.

80. Harvey Jones, *Mathews: Masterpieces of the California Decorative Style*, Oakland: Oakland Museum, 1972, pp. 77, 35. Like Keith, the Mathews exhibited their work at the Bohemian Club and their paintings were featured prominently at the 1915 Panama Pacific International Exposition, where Lucia received a silver medal (see pp. 65, 23). The Bohemian Club, a San Francisco-based men's organization founded in 1872 by a group of writers, expanded over time to include prominent businessmen and artists. An annual celebration took place in a campsite among the redwoods of northern California. For more on the Bohemian Club, see Longstreth, *On the Edge of the World*, p. 111; William H. Smith and James J. Gill, *A Chronicle of Our Early Years, Commemorating the 75th Anniversary of the Founding of the Bohemian Club of San Francisco*, San Francisco: Bohemian Club and Grabhorn Press, 1947.

81. Jones, *Mathews*, p. 67.

82. William Bade, *The Life and Letters of John Muir*, Boston: Houghton Mifflin, 1924, pp. 207–08.

83. Redwood Empire building, Golden Gate International Exposition, 1936–39, folder 78b, Maybeck Collection, EDA, UCB.

84. Jordy, *American Buildings*, p. 300.

85. Lumbermen's Association building/House of Hoo-Hoo (hereafter simply House of Hoo-Hoo) job file, letter to Rodeny Burns, Eureka, Calif., 28 Mar 1914, Maybeck Collection, EDA, UCB.

86. House of Hoo-Hoo job file, letter to building committee, 21 January 1915, and earlier letter to R. A. Hiscox, committee's chair, 24 July 1914, Maybeck collection, EDA, UCB.

87. Planting list for House of Hoo-Hoo, Carl Purdy, landscape architect, no date, House of Hoo-Hoo job file, Maybeck Collection, EDA, UCB. Purdy's practice was located in Ukiah and he seems to have been a nursery operator as well as designer. According to his stationery letterhead, his nursery specialized in high-quality Dutch bulbs and in the "best hardy and native ferns." The list is covered with handwritten notations by Maybeck, who clearly collaborated with Purdy on plant selections. "Bedding out" was the common nineteenth-century practice of creating large, showy floral displays in contained areas.

88. Macomber, *Jewel City*, p. 25.

89. "Lumberman's Building," *Western Architect*, September 1915, p. 25.

90. For example, see Maybeck's description of his Palace of Fine Arts ground plan and its resemblance to a golden brooch in *Palace of Fine Arts and Lagoon*, 1915, as excerpted in Woodbridge, *Bernard Maybeck*, p. 102.

91. Principia College drawings, Aeroplane perspective of general plan for Principia College, 13 April 1931, folder 178; Principia sunken garden, folder 177; general plan of study of Principia, 238/2 in folder 160, Maybeck Collection, EDA, UCB.

92. Palace of Fine Arts job file, Maybeck Collection, EDA, UCB.

93. Jacomena Maybeck, *Maybeck: The Family View*, Berkeley: Berkeley Architectural Heritage Association, 1980, p. 12.

94. Cardwell, *Maybeck*, pp. 21–22.

95. For Maybeck's drawing of the mission restoration, see tube 22, California Missions, San Carlos, Carmel, no date; for his letter to Father Mestres, 12 January 1920, see folder 36, both in Maybeck Collection, EDA, UCB.

96. Rita Carroll, "Bernard R. Maybeck's Bird's Eye View of a University of California Hospital," *University of California San Francisco Alumni News 4*, no. 4, Fall 1985, p. 10.

97. Unfortunately, lack of funding ended the project and the Italianate landscape design shown in Maybeck's rendering; Louis Hobart, the architect of Grace Cathedral, designed the hospital in 1917, using the pavilion model in his plan for the hospital as well as some of Maybeck's lighting ideas.

98. Kenneth Cardwell asserted that Maybeck was the primary architect on the gymnasium (1989 correspondence with the author) and used the water gardens at Nîmes as a prototype for his design. Cardwell, *Maybeck*, p. 199; but in Sally Woodbridge's undocumented comment, Maybeck's involvement with the final building form was so limited that he did not know where the bathrooms were on opening day. Woodbridge, *Bernard Maybeck*, p. 87.

99. Hearst Gymnasium job file, letter to John Gregg, 9 January 1926, Maybeck Collection, EDA, UCB.

100. Hearst Gymnasium job file, letter from Gregg, 7 Oct 1926, Maybeck Collection, EDA, UCB.

101. Hillside Club (residence sketches for booklet), no date, Maybeck Collection, EDA, UCB.

102. For the site plan see tube 26, "Woodside Oaks," Maybeck collection, EDA, UCB.

103. Many California architects experimented with residential designs that involved a degree of open-air living. A famed southern Californian example is Rudolf Schindler's Kings Road residence in Los Angeles, which had outdoor sleeping areas on the roofs, sliding wall panels that opened rooms to the outdoors, and an outdoor cooking area. In Berkeley, the most famous example is probably the "Temple of the Wings" designed by A. Randolph Monro for the Charles Boynton family. Though significantly remodeled, the original structure contained almost no solid walls, substituting canvases hung between columns to keep out the rain and wind.

104. Jordy, *American Buildings*, pp. 304–5.

105. Macomber, *Jewel City*, p. 102. And on the fair's phoenixlike aspect, see Marjorie M. Dobkin, "A Twenty-Five-Million-Dollar Mirage," in Burton Benedict, ed., *The Anthropology of World's Fairs: San Francisco's Pan Pacific International Exposition of 1915*, Berkeley: Lowie Museum of Anthropology; London: Scolari Press, 1983, pp. 66–67.

106. Louis J. Stellmann, *That Was a Dream Worth Building*, San Francisco: H. S. Crocker, Publishers, 1916, p. 20.

107. Macomber, *Jewel City*, pp. 19, 20; on this objective see p. 15.

108. Strawberry Canyon Bath House job file, letter of 21 December 1910, Maybeck Collection, EDA, UCB. A letter in the project's office file written by one of the regents requests that the architect make suggestions for planting and gardening around the pool, though no drawings exist for this planting.

109. Quoted in Macomber, *Jewel City*, p. 102.

110. Keeler, *Simple Home*, p. 8.

111. Gray Brechin, "Sailing to Byzantium," in Benedict, *Anthropology of World's Fairs*, pp. 106, 107.

112. Van Zanten, "Architectural Polychromy,"in Middleton, ed., *The Beaux-Arts*, p. 213.

113. Ibid., pp. 213–15.

114. Maybeck did not design but may have consulted on the courtyard and garden formed by the addition of Henry Gutterson's Sunday school. Its present layout is probably the result of work completed in the 1960s.

115. See drawing titled "First Science Church, Berkeley, Landscape Planting Plan," no date, The Bancroft Library, University of California, Berkeley.

116. Interview with Jacomena Maybeck, 11 January 1989.

117. First Church of Christ, Scientist, Berkeley, job file, letters from Maybeck, 1 April 1938 and 5 January 1937, Maybeck Collection, EDA, UCB.

118. Cardwell, *Maybeck*, p. 88.

119. Jacomena Maybeck, *The Family View*, p. 29

120. Jordy, *American Buildings*, p. 300.

121. Palace of Fine Arts job file, Maybeck Collection, EDA, UCB.

122. Reyner Banham, "The Plot Against Bernard Maybeck," *Journal of the Society of Architectural Historians 43*, no. 1, March 1984, p. 36.

123. Donald McLaren, "Landscape Gardening at the Exposition," *Western Architect*, September 1915, p. 14.

124. Louis Christian Mullgardt, *The Architecture and Landscape Gardening of the Exposition*, San Francisco: Paul Elder, 1915, p. 168.

125. Cardwell, *Maybeck*, p. 149.

126. Palace of Fine Arts job file, Maybeck Collection, EDA, UCB.

127. Mullgardt, *Architecture and Landscape Gardening*, p. 8. Jules Guérin was director of color for the Panama Pacific International Exposition of 1915 and a prominent muralist in North America during the first decades of the twentieth century. He also created the renderings for Daniel Burnham's 1909 Plan of Chicago. For more on Guérin, see Jules Guérin, *Master Delineator: An Exhibition*, Houston: University of Houston Press, 1983; and Jules Vallée Guérin and Maxfield Parrish, *A Collection of Color Prints by Jules Guérin and Maxfield Parrish*, Cleveland: J. H. Jansen, 1900.

128. Cardwell, *Maybeck*, p. 198. In some of Maybeck's drawings, the gymnasium's swimming pool served as a forecourt to the complex.

129. Brechin, "Sailing to Byzantium," in Benedict, ed., *Anthropology of World's Fairs*, p. 110.

130. Drawings titled "Twin Peaks Planning," no date, folder 230; "Twin Peaks Auditorium, San Francisco, CA" no date, tube 115; and one titled "Berkeley Harbor," no date, tube 19, Maybeck Collection, EDA, UCB.

131. Daniel Burnham, *Report on a Plan for San Francisco*, San Francisco: Sunset Press, 1905, p. 8.

132. Ibid., p. 132.

133. Ibid., p. 183.

134. Shipounoff, introduction, p. xxxvi. For more on Maybeck's designs for San Francisco, see Paolo Polledri, ed., *Visionary San Francisco*, New York: Neues Publishing; Munich: Prestal, 1990.

135. Here Maybeck's method departed from his training, since drawing in perspective was a rare occurrence at the École des Beaux-Arts. My thanks to Richard Longstreth for bringing this point to my attention.

136. Principia College files, Maybeck Collection, EDA, UCB.

BIBLIOGRAPHY

Archives

Bernard Maybeck Collection, Environmental Design Archives of the University of California, Berkeley (online catalog at www.ced.berkeley.edu/cedarchives/use.html)

The Online Archive of California (www.oac.cdlib.org/)

Historical and primary sources

Adams, Charles Gibbs. "Gardens for the Stars." *Saturday Evening Post*, March 2, 1940, pp. 18–19, 74.

André, Édouard. *L'art des jardins: traité général de la composition des parcs et jardins*. 1889. Reprint; Marseille: Laffitte, 1983.

Blomfield, Reginald. *The Formal Garden in England*. 3rd ed. London: Macmillan, 1901. First published with coauthor Inigo F. Thomas in 1892 by Macmillan. Page references are to 3rd ed.

Burnham, Daniel. *Report on a Plan for San Francisco*. San Francisco: Sunset Press, 1905.

Gill, Irving. "The Home of the Future: The New Architecture of the West: Small Homes for a Great Country, Number Four." *The Craftsman* 30, no. 2, May 1916, pp. 140–51.

Guérin, Jules Vallée, and Maxfield Parrish. *A Collection of Color Prints by Jules Guérin and Maxfield Parrish*. Cleveland: J. H. Jansen, 1900.

Haverlin, Carl. *The Romance of Transportation in California and Story of the Packard Building*. Oakland: Earle C. Anthony, 1928.

Hegemann, Werner. *Report on a City Plan for the Municipalities of Oakland and Berkeley*. Oakland and Berkeley: Municipal Governments of Oakland and Berkeley, 1915.

Hegemann, Werner, and Elbert Peets. *American Vitruvius: An Architect's Handbook of Civic Art*. New York: Architectural Book Publishing, 1922.

Hillside Club Yearbook, 1906–7. The Bancroft Library, University of California, Berkeley.

Hopkins, Una Nixson. "The Development of Domestic Architecture on the Pacific Coast." *The Craftsman* 13, no. 4, January 1908, pp. 450–57.

John Gregg: A Half-Century of Landscape Architecture. Berkeley: Regional Oral History Office, 1965.

Keeler, Charles. *Bird Notes Afield*. San Francisco: Paul Elder, 1907.

———. *To California and Back, a Book of Practical Information for Travelers to the Pacific*. New York: Doubleday, Page, 1903.

———. *San Francisco and Thereabout*. San Francisco: California Promotion Committee, 1902.

———. *San Francisco through Earthquake and Fire*. San Francisco: Paul Elder, 1906.

———. *Sequoia Sonnets*. Berkeley: Sign of the Live Oak Publishers, 1919.

"Lumberman's Building." *Western Architect*, September 1915, p. 25.

McLaren, Donald. "Landscape Gardening at the Exposition." *Western Architect*, September 1915, 14.

McLaren, John. *Gardening in California: Landscape and Flower*. San Francisco: A. M. Robertson, 1908 and 1914.

Macomber, Ben. *The Jewel City*. San Francisco: John H. Williams, 1915.

Maybeck, Bernard. *Palace of Fine Arts and Lagoon*. San Francisco: Paul Elder, 1915.

Mullgardt, Louis Christian. *The Architecture and Landscape Gardening of the Exposition*. San Francisco: Paul Elder, 1915.

Platt, Charles. *Italian Gardens*. 1884. Reprint; Portland, Ore.: Saga/Timber Press, 1993.

Robinson, William. *The Wild Garden, or Our Groves and Shrubberies Made Beautiful*. London: John Murray, 1870.

Sedding, John. *Garden-Craft Old and New*. London: K. Paul, Trench, Trübner, 1892.

Smith, William H., and James J. Gill. *A Chronicle of Our Early Years, Commemorating the 75th Anniversary* of the *Founding of the Bohemian Club of San Francisco*. San Francisco: Bohemian Club and Grabhorn Press, 1947.

Stellmann, Louis J. *That Was a Dream Worth Building*. San Francisco: H. S. Crocker, Publishers, 1916.

Secondary sources

Aguar, Charles E., and Berdeana Aguar. *Wrightscapes: Frank Lloyd Wright's Landscape Designs*. New York: McGraw-Hill, 2002.

Bade, William. *The Life and Letters of John Muir*. Boston: Houghton Mifflin, 1924.

Banham, Reyner. "The Plot Against Bernard Maybeck." *Journal of the Society of Architectural Historians* 43, no. 1, March 1984, pp. 33–37.

Benedict, Burton, ed. *The Anthropology of World's Fairs: San Francisco's Pan Pacific International Exhibition of 1915*. Berkeley: Lowie Museum of Anthropology; London: Scolari Press, 1983.

Birnbaum, Charles A., and Robin Karson, eds. *Pioneers of Landscape Design*. New York: McGraw-Hill, 2000.

Bloomfield, Anne. "The Evolution of a Landscape: Charles Sumner Greene's Designs for Green Gables." *Journal of the Society of Architectural Historians*, September 1988, pp. 231–44.

Boutelle, Sarah Holmes. *Julia Morgan, Architect*. New York: Abbeville, 1988.

Brechin, Gray. *Imperial San Francisco: Urban Power, Earthly Ruin*. Berkeley: University of California Press, 1999.

———. "Sailing to Byzantium." In Burton Benedict, ed., *The Anthropology of World's Fairs: San Francisco's Pan Pacific International Exhibition of 1915*, pp. 94–113.

Brown, Jane. *Gardens of a Golden Afternoon*. New York: Penguin Books, 1982.

Brown, Janet Lynn. "Charles Sumner and Henry Mather Greene, Architects: The Integration of House and Garden, Southern California, 1889–1914." Master's thesis, University of California, Berkeley, 1988.

Cardwell, Kenneth. *Bernard Maybeck: Artisan, Architect, Artist*. Salt Lake City: Peregrine Smith Books, 1977.

Carroll, Rita. "Bernard R. Maybeck's Bird's Eye View of a University of California Hospital." *University of California San Francisco Alumni News* 4, Fall 1985, p. 10.

Clark, Robert Judson. "Louis Christian Mullgardt." In Robert W. Winter, ed., *Toward a Simpler Way of Life: The Arts and Crafts Architects of California*, Berkeley: University of California Press, 1997, pp. 41–50.

Cornelius, Brother Fidelis. *Keith, Old Master of California*. New York: G. P. Putnam's Sons, 1942.

Craig, Robert M. *Bernard Maybeck at Principia College: The Art and Craft of Building*. Layton, Utah: Gibbs Smith Publisher, 2004.

Cronon, William. "Inconstant Unity: The Passion of Frank Lloyd Wright." In Terence Riley, ed., *Frank Lloyd Wright: Architect*. New York: Museum of Modern Art, 1994. Pp. 8–31.

David DeLong, ed., *Frank Lloyd Wright: Designs for an American Landscape, 1922–1932*. New York: Harry Abrams, 1996.

Dobkin, Marjorie M. "A Twenty-Five-Million-Dollar Mirage." In Burton Benedict, ed., *The Anthropology of World's Fairs: San Francisco's Pan Pacific International Exhibition of 1915*, pp. 66–93.

Domer, Dennis, ed. *Alfred Caldwell: The Life and Work of a Prairie School Landscape Architect*. Baltimore: Johns Hopkins University Press, 1997.

Drexler, Arthur, ed. *The Architecture of the École des Beaux-Arts*. New York: Museum of Modern Art and MIT Press, 1977.

Festing, Sally. *Gertrude Jekyll*. London: Penguin Books, 1991.

Freudenheim, Leslie Mandelson, and Elisabeth Sussman. *Building with Nature: Roots of the San Francisco Bay Tradition*. Santa Barbara: Peregrine Smith, 1974.

Gebhard, David. *Lutah Maria Riggs: A Woman in California Architecture.* Santa Barbara: Capra Press, 1992.

Grese, Robert. *Jens Jensen: Maker of Natural Parks and Gardens.* Baltimore: Johns Hopkins University Press, 1992.

Griswold, Mac, and Eleanor Weller. *The Golden Age of American Gardens: Proud Owners, Private Estates, 1890–1940.* New York: Harry N. Abrams, 1992.

Guérin, Jules Vallée. *Jules Guérin, Master Delineator: An Exhibition.* Houston: University of Houston Press, 1983.

Harris, Dianne. "Architecture and the Garden: The Landscape Designs of Bernard Maybeck." Master's thesis, University of California, Berkeley, 1989.

———. "Landscape in Context." In Mirka Benes and Dianne Harris, eds., *Villas and Gardens in Early Modern Italy and France.* New York: Cambridge University Press, 2001, pp. 16–28.

———. "Making Gardens in the Athens of the West: Bernard Maybeck and the San Francisco Bay Region Tradition in Landscape and Garden Design." In Therese O'Malley and Marc Treib, eds., *Regional Garden Design*, pp. 43–68.

———. "Making Your Private World: Modern Landscape Architecture and House Beautiful, 1945–1965." In Marc Treib, ed., *The Architecture of Landscape, 1940–1960.* Philadelphia: University of Pennsylvania Press, 2002, pp. 180–205.

———. "Maybeck's Landscapes." *Journal of Garden History* 10, no. 2, July–September 1990, pp. 145–61.

Hawley, Henry. "An Italianate Garden by Greene and Greene." *Journal of Decorative and Propaganda Arts* 2, Summer–Fall 1986, pp. 32–45.

Helmreich, Anne. *The English Garden and National Identity: The Competing Styles of Garden Design, 1870–1914.* New York: Cambridge University Press, 2002.

Hitchmough, Wendy. *Arts and Crafts Gardens.* New York: Rizzoli, 1997.

Hjalmerson, Birgitta. *Artful Players: Artistic Life in Early San Francisco.* New York: Princeton Architectural Press, 2001.

Howett, Catherine. "Frank Lloyd Wright and American Residential Landscaping." *Landscape* 26, no. 1, 1982, pp. 45–57.

Hunt, John Dixon. *Gardens and the Picturesque: Studies in the History of Landscape Architecture.* Cambridge, Mass.: MIT Press, 1992.

———. *The Picturesque Garden in Europe.* London: Thames and Hudson, 2002.

Hunt, John Dixon, and Peter Willis, eds. *The Genius of the Place: The English Landscape Garden, 1620–1820.* New York: Harper, 1975.

Imbert, Dorothée. *The Modernist Garden in France.* New Haven: Yale University Press, 1993.

Jacques, Annie. "The Programmes of the Architectural Section of the Ecole des Beaux-Arts, 1918–1914." In Robin Middleton, ed., *The Beaux-Arts and Nineteenth-Century French Architecture*, pp. 58–65.

Jones, Harvey L. *Mathews: Masterpieces of the California Decorative Style.* Oakland: Oakland Museum, 1972.

Jordy, William H. *American Buildings and Their Architects: Progressive and Academic Ideals at the Turn of the Twentieth Century.* Oxford: Oxford University Press, 1972.

Karson, Robin. *The Muses of Gwinn.* New York: Harry N. Abrams, 1996.

Leonard, John William, ed. *Woman's Who's Who of America, 1914–1915.* New York: American Commonwealth, 1914.

Levine, Neil. *The Architecture of Frank Lloyd Wright.* Princeton: Princeton University Press, 1997.

———. "The Book and the Building: Hugo's Theory of Architecture and Labrouste's Bibliothèque Ste-Geneviève." In Robin Middleton, ed., *The Beaux-Arts and Nineteenth-Century French Architecture,* pp. 138–73.

———. " The Romantic Idea of Architectural Legibility: Henri Labrouste and the Neo-Grec." In Arthur Drexler, ed., *The Architecture of the École des Beaux-Arts,* pp. 325–416.

Longstreth, Richard. *On the Edge of the World: Four Architects in San Francisco at the Turn of the Century.* Cambridge, Mass.: Architectural History Foundation and MIT Press, 1983.

McClung, William Alexander. *Landscapes of Desire: Anglo Mythologies of Los Angeles.* Berkeley: University of California Press, 2000.

McCoy, Esther. *Five California Architects.* New York: Reinhold Publications, 1960.

Makinson, Randell. *Greene and Greene.* Salt Lake City: Gibbs Smith, 2001.

MacPhail, Elizabeth C. *Kate Sessions: Pioneer Horticulturalist.* San Diego: San Diego Historical Society, 1976.

Maybeck, Jacomena. *Maybeck: The Family View.* Berkeley: Berkeley Architectural Heritage Association, 1980.

Middleton, Robin, ed. *The Beaux-Arts and Nineteenth-Century French Architecture.* Cambridge, Mass.: MIT Press, 1982.

Morgan, Keith. *Charles A. Platt: The Artist as Architect.* New York: Architectural History Foundation and MIT Press, 1985.

Neuhaus, Eugen. *William Keith: The Man and the Artist.* Berkeley: University of California Press, 1938.

Nevins, Deborah. "Morris, Ruskin, and the English Flower Garden." *Antiques* 129, no. 5, June 1986, pp. 1256–65.

O'Malley, Therese, and Marc Treib, eds. *Regional Garden Design in the United States.* Washington, D.C.: Dumbarton Oaks, 1995.

Polledri, Paolo, ed. *Visionary San Francisco.* New York: Neues Publishing; Munich: Prestal, 1990.

Ranney, Victoria Post, ed. *The Papers of Frederick Law Olmsted, Volume 5, The California Frontier, 1863–65.* Baltimore: Johns Hopkins University Press, 1990.

Roberts, Jan, ed. *Avalon: Landscape and Harmony: Walter Burley Griffin, Alexander Stewart Jolly, and Harry Ruskin Stowe*. Avalon Beach: Ruskin Rowe Press, 1999.

Shipounoff, Dimitri. Introduction to *The Simple Home*, by Charles Keeler. Santa Barbara: Peregrine Smith, 1979, pp. i–xlvi.

Spirn, Anne Whiston. "Frank Lloyd Wright: Architect of Landscape." In David DeLong, ed., *Frank Lloyd Wright: Designs for an American Landscape, 1922–1932*. New York: Harry Abrams, 1996, pp. 135–69.

Starr, Kevin. *Americans and the California Dream, 1850–1915*. Salt Lake City: Peregrine Smith, 1981.

Stevens, Mark. "An Architect Is Chosen." *Principia Pilot*, November 19, 1971.

Streatfield, David. *California Gardens: Creating a New Eden*. New York: Abbeville Press, 1994.

Tishler, William, ed. *Midwestern Landscape Architecture*. Urbana: University of Illinois Press, 2000.

Treib, Marc. "Aspects of Regionality and the Modern(ist) Garden in California." In O'Malley and Treib, eds., *Regional Garden Design*, pp. 43–68.

———, ed. *An Everyday Modernism: The Houses of William Wurster*. Berkeley: University of California Press, 1995.

Van Zanten, David. "Architectural Polychromy: Life in Architecture." In Robin Middleton, ed., *The Beaux-Arts and Nineteenth-Century French Architecture*, pp. 196–215.

———. "Architectural Composition at the École des Beaux-Arts, from Charles Percier to Charles Garnier," in Drexler, ed., *The Architecture of the École des Beaux-Arts*, pp. 111–324.

———. ed. *The Nature of Frank Lloyd Wright*. Chicago: University of Chicago Press, 1988.

Vernon, Christopher. "Walter Burley Griffin, Landscape Architect." In Creese and Garner, eds., *The Midwest in American Architecture*. Urbana: University of Illinois Press, 1991, pp. 217–30.

Wheeler, Ann. "The Maybeck Challenge, The Maybeck Answer." *Principia Pilot*, November 19, 1971.

Woodbridge, Sally. *Bernard Maybeck: Visionary Architect*. New York: Abbeville Press, 1992.

Worster, Donald. *Rivers of Empire: Water, Aridity, and the Growth of the American West*. New York: Oxford University Press, 1985.

Wright, Frank Lloyd. "Concerning Landscape Architecture." In Bruce Pfeiffer, ed., *Frank Lloyd Wright: Collected Writings, vol. 1*. New York: Rizzoli, 1992, pp. 54–57

Interviews and lectures

Clark, Robert Judson. Lecture at the School of Architecture, University of Illinois, Urbana-Champaign, 19 November 2002.

Jacomena Maybeck, 11 January 1989, Berkeley, California.

BERNARD MAYBECK COLLECTION

Donated in 1956 by the architect, the Bernard Maybeck collection spans the years 1897–1956 (bulk 1902–1939) and includes personal papers and correspondence, office and project files, drawings, and photographs. The collection is divided into nine series: Personal Papers, Professional Papers, Office Records, Project Records, University of California, Expositions, Principia College, Art and Artifacts, and Additional Donations. The Personal Papers include autobiographical information, correspondence, creative writings by Maybeck, photographs, medical records, and a scrapbook created by Maybeck's daughter, Kerna. The Professional Papers contain correspondence, writings, and speeches by Maybeck, committee work, awards, and publications on the architect and his work. The Office Records series comprises administrative materials, financial records, and an array of product literature. The largest series, Project Records, consists of files, photographs, and drawings for over 250 of Maybeck's residential, commercial, recreational, and religious projects in the San Francisco Bay Area and California.

Three other series also feature Maybeck's design work. The first contains project files, photographs, and drawings for the University of California at Berkeley—including materials on the Phoebe Hearst Competition for the plan of the university and the Faculty Club. The second project-related series documents Maybeck's work for two important California expositions—the Panama Pacific International Exposition of 1915 and the Golden Gate International Exposition of 1939. The final project-related series documents Maybeck's designs for Principia College—a college for the Church of Christ, Scientist located in Elsah, Illinois—and the voluminous correspondence between Maybeck and Frederic Morgan, president of the college.

The final two series—Art and Artifacts, and Additional Donations—include a table designed by Maybeck and a piece of bubblestone, an experimental building material he helped develop and favored.

Unfortunately, the Maybeck Collection contains few records from his years of study at the École des Beaux-Arts in Paris. No records document his work as an instructor at the University of California, nor his involvement with the founding of the Department of Architecture on the Berkeley campus. Also absent are personal papers and professional records lost in either the 1906 San Francisco earthquake and fire (Maybeck's office at that time was in San Francisco) or the 1923 Berkeley fire that destroyed his home.

A complete inventory of the collection is available on the Environmental Design Archives Web site:
http://www.ced.berkeley.edu/cedarchives/profiles/maybeck.htm

Mailing Address
Environmental Design Archives
230 Wurster Hall #1820
University of California
Berkeley, CA 94720-1820

Office and Reading Room
280 Wurster Hall

Telephone: 510.642.5124
Fax: 510.642.2824
Email: archives@socrates.berkeley.edu
URL: www.ced/berkeley.edu/cedarchives/

INDEX